BEDTIME with the SAINTS

FR. FRANK LEE, CSSR

with new stories by Christine Watkins

©2025 Queen of Peace Media
All rights reserved.
www.QueenofPeaceMedia.com
Novato, California

No part of this book may be used, reproduced, put online, on video, stored in a retrieval system, or transmitted by any means—written, electronic, recording, photocopying or otherwise—without written permission from the publisher, except in the case of brief quotations embodied in reviews.

Cover design by Tianna Williams (www.sacredartbytianna.com)
Drawings by Winendra Adi

Books may be purchased in quantity by contacting the publisher directly at orders@queenofpeacemedia.com.

ISBN: 978-1-947701-26-7

CONTENTS

	Acknowledgments	5
1	SAINT JOSEPH — The Father Who Brought Up Jesus	7
2	SAINT PAUL — The Man God Knocked to the Ground	15
3	SAINT KATERI TEKAKWITHA — The Lily of the Mohawks	19
4	SAINT PATRICK — The Man Who Won Ireland for Our Lord	33
5	SERVANT OF GOD JULIA GREELEY — God's Secret Night Angel	41
6	SAINT FRANCIS DE SALES — The Sword Fighter with a Temper	47
7	SAINT EDMUND CAMPION — The Martyr They Chased All Over England	53
8	SAINT JOAN OF ARC — The Girl Who Won the Fight for France	59
9	SAINT GERARD MAJELLA — The Skinny Kid Who Made It Big	65
10	LUIGI AND MARIA BELTRAME QUATTROCCHI — A Match Made in Heaven	73

11	SAINT ANTHONY OF PADUA — He Had His Own Tree House	81
12	SAINT CLEMENT MARIA HOFBAUER — The Baker Who Would Not Quit	89
13	SAINT BENEDICT LABRE — The Homeless Man Who Tramped into Heaven	99
14	SAINT MARTIN DE PORRES — The Barber Who Became a Saint	107
15	SAINT CATHERINE LABOURÉ — She Ate a Relic and Saw Mary	115
16	VENERABLE FRANCIS XAVIER NGUYỄN VĂN THUẬN — Captivity Could Not Contain Him	127
17	SAINT JOHN BOSCO — Love Him, Love His Dog	145
18	CARLO ACUTIS —The First Millennial Saint	157
	APPENDIX	181
	NOTES	182
	WHO WROTE WHAT	188
	OTHER BOOKS BY QUEEN OF PEACE MEDIA	191

ACKNOWLEDGMENTS

I am humbly indebted to the late Fr. Frank Lee, whose original stories live on in this work. I remain deeply grateful for his wit, storytelling genius, and love for God's children. Four special people graciously gave their time and talent to help shape six additional stories: heartfelt thanks to my son Christian, my husband John, Tim Hannie, and Verna Versperien. Finally, I extend my sincere respect and gratitude to Jason Punsalan, whose creative formatting, artistic eye, and extraordinary patience made this book possible.

1

SAINT JOSEPH

- The Father Who Brought Up Jesus -

How do you feel when you have been running around all day, and your mother finally catches up with you, throws you in the tub, and you get all clean and dressed, and then you sit in a nice, cool room and look at your most favorite picture book? Everything is quiet and peaceful, with a soft light around the edges.

That is St. Joseph. When you start thinking about him, you close the door on all kinds of things, like cold wars and hot wars, atom bombs, and newspapers full of robbery and murder. You just sort of see a tall, quiet man leaning over his carpenter's bench. His hair is getting a little gray around the edges, and the sweat glistens on his brow as he straightens up.

"Mary, where's the Infant?"

"Oh, goodness!" says Our Lady from the kitchen. "He was here just a minute ago. I thought he crawled in to watch you. Wait a minute. Here he is. Oh . . . he can't get up the doorsteps. Come here, you poor Darling." And this very beautiful woman swishes up her tiny God in her arms and gives him a good, sound kiss.

The big man smiles. God has made him protector of these two. They love him, obey him. Of course, he adores them and would die for them with a song on his lips.

This is Joseph. He did not know it, but his name would be in our Bible someday. Oh, the Bible

would not say very much about him. It would just tell us that God chose him to be the husband of the Blessed Virgin and the foster father and guardian of our Lord. But the Bible does say one special thing about him. It calls him *a just man*. Do you know what that means? No, it does not mean that he kept from cheating and paid his bills. It means that, all right, but it means worlds besides that. In the days when the Bible was written, the word *just* meant *good* and *honorable* and *pure* and *loyal*. And that will do for a perfect picture of St. Joseph.

"Mary, where's the Baby? Forgive me, Mary. I know he is sleeping there, but I am all confused. You must wake him and dress him. We have to go on a long journey, Mary. The Father in heaven sent an angel to me this night to warn us that King Herod wants to kill the young Jesus. Quick, my dear, there is no time to lose. I will get the donkey ready. Mary . . . the angel said that we must go all the way to Egypt."

I guess there were tears in Mary's eyes that night. After all, a mother is a mother, and her baby is her baby, even though He is God's Son, too. Nowadays, when a mother takes her baby out for a weekend holiday, she packs the back of the car with clothes and blankets and thingamajigs, until there is hardly room for the baby. But Mary had to leave almost everything behind. Just take a blanket or two, some clothing, and then hurry out into the cold night with her precious Child in her arms. Believe me, our Lady felt pretty blue that night, to say the least.

But poor St. Joseph! He must have felt still worse. After all, you can get a little nervous taking care of God's Son for Him, with God sort of watching over your shoulder to see how you are doing. But, of course, this trip was God's idea, and Joseph had plenty of trust in God. And then there was the Blessed Mother, too, whom he was supposed to be protecting, and here he was, leading her out on a donkey, at midnight, through miles and miles of King Herod's country.

So, he plodded along, while he remembered another time that he had led her on a donkey. It was that wonderful first Christmas. Actually, it had not been so wonderful at first. By the time he got to Bethlehem that day, there had been no place to stay. You see, the Roman emperor had conquered Bethlehem and Jerusalem and everything, and he wanted to know just how many people he had conquered, so they all had to go back to their hometown and sign up. It seems that Bethlehem was full of old home towners that evening, and Joseph just could not find rooms anywhere. He must have felt like lots of us do sometimes—that we just can't do anything right. There he was! He was supposed to be protecting Mary, and he could not even find her a cot. And along with that, the Infant would soon be born, and here he was, finally leading Mary and the donkey out to an old stable for the night.

But it had all ended so beautifully. The lovely Baby Jesus was born into the world, and the angels sang *Glory be to God in the Highest*, as if they had written it themselves. (Well, maybe they did, at that.)

Tonight was a lot different from that Christmas night. All the way to Egypt! Not 10 million angels singing a glorious welcome to the Christ Child, but just one angel with those cold words, "Take the Child and his Mother, and fly into Egypt." Not the tiny Prince of Peace sitting on the royal throne of this Mother's lap, receiving the wonderful gifts of the three kings, but a whimpering little Baby in terrible flight from a king whose heart was bad.

And now Joseph wondered what was ahead of them. Could he get a job in Egypt? What language did they speak over there? Would he find a place for them to live? He was not a very proud protector that night. He was only Joseph, the just man, putting his chest to the night wind, wiping away a tear with his sleeve. The cold air can string quite a bit, Joseph, or . . . maybe you are crying just a little, too?

"Mary, where's the Boy?"
The sweet years of infancy are gone now. Mary and Joseph had taken our young Lord to the great city of Jerusalem so that they could go to the temple for a great feast day.

And now it was the old story again. "Mary, where is the Boy?"

"Oh, my goodness, Joseph! I thought he was with you."

They were on their way back home from the temple in Jerusalem, and each one had thought that Jesus was with the other one. Once more Joseph, the *protector*, began to wonder what the Father in heaven thought of him for losing his only Son somewhere back in the big city.

Poor Joseph! Back he goes, searching everywhere for the Child, and now and then he looks at Mary out of the corner of his eye, sort of wondering what she thinks of this big protector of hers, who could not keep that eye on one Child. Surely Mary knew it was not Joseph's fault, but just the same she was worried. She knew her Child was very obedient and thoughtful, and so there must be something pretty serious that made Him stay back in Jerusalem.

And it was pretty serious. Oh, they found the Christ Child all right, explaining the Bible to some old gentlemen who were listening with their mouths wide open at the great wisdom of this young

Boy. But the serious part was His answer when His parents told him that they had been searching for Him with great sorrow. Our Lord looked at them and said:

Did you not know that I must be about my Father's business?

And Mary looked into His eyes. Yes, she knew. She had known since the day she had told the angel Gabriel that she would be the Mother of this young God. And St. Joseph bowed his head. Yes, he knew. He felt that this was not their Boy anymore. He had always known it had to come, but, oh, how deeply it hurt! The heavenly Father had given them this Christ Child for a while, but now this Child's mind was running ahead to the day when he would begin to work at his Father's business. And that business was to save the world. He could not belong only to Mary and Joseph anymore; He belonged to the people; He belonged to the endless millions of Christians who would follow Him even to death; He belonged to Calvary and His Cross.

Quietly they all returned home.

"Mary, where is He?"

"He is here, Joseph."

"I am here, My father."

"It is well. My eyes fade, my dear Jesus, my dear Mary. Let me look upon you for this last time. Was ever a man so blessed at his death to be surrounded by his Child, who is God's Son, and his spouse, who is his Queen? Ours was a poor life, my dear Ones, but, oh, how rich was I to live that life with You! And so shall all men and women and children be rich for all time to come if they humbly seek to live their lives with You. It is well. The heavenly Father has honored his poor old servant, for

I was the first of millions to find Jesus through Mary.

"I am at peace. But I stop a moment at the final gate and look back through the years. Do you remember that Christmas, Mary? That song the angels sang? I hear it again, Mary, I hear it again!"

"And the Egypt years. The Nazareth years. Did you know I was pretty nervous, dear Jesus, when I saw my young God pick up a saw for the first time? Oh, but I feared for Your fingers. And then I would say to myself, 'Joseph, do you realize that you just spent the last half hour telling the Master of the world how to saw a piece of wood?'

"And the little donkey. Hah! Between us, we managed to carry a very sweet burden."

A smile spread over the just man's face, and the carpenter's rough hands grew forever quiet in the hands of Jesus and Mary.

No wonder that he is the patron of a happy death.

Now go to sleep, quietly.

2

SAINT PAUL

- The Man God Knocked to the Ground -

Most likely, dear children, you have heard the word MISSIONARY. Tonight, we are going to talk about the greatest missionary of them all—St. Paul.

St. Paul was lucky because he knew St. Peter and the other special helpers of Jesus; he spent time with them and heard them talk about the things Our Lord did when he was alive. So, St. Paul should know what he is talking about.

At first St. Paul did not like Our Lord. (At that time, he did not actually know who our Lord was and St. Paul wasn't a saint yet.) So, he kept on hurting people who loved Our Lord.

Well, anyway, he was on the way to a city called Damascus, one day, to hurt some more Christians, and that was the day that Jesus made up His mind that He had had just about enough of this. So, Jesus knocked St. Paul onto the ground, maybe even off his horse, and a bright light from heaven flashed in the sky, in order to put some sense into his head. (Of course, St. Paul, as I told you, was not yet a saint.)

Also, our Lord made St. Paul blind.

But our Lord loved St. Paul, so he gave him back his eyesight and he could see again. He gave him another kind of sight, too, and then St. Paul could see that everybody should become a Christian and should get to understand that Jesus was God and that they should all love Him. From then on, St. Paul really worked hard for Our Lord. His life had a lot of adventure, like Spiderman, but

without all the swinging around and shooting sticky webs out of your wrists.

Well, anyhow, just to give you an idea, St. Paul was shipwrecked three times, and he still came up looking for souls for our Lord. About eight or nine times, he stood there while they beat him with a whip; but St. Paul went through it all, because he figured that this was the price he had to pay for working for Our Lord.

Most Likely, St. Paul's toughest time was when those people followed him into that man's house in Damascus to kill him. But St. Paul got away, because the man in this house loved Jesus, and he let St. Paul down from the house in a basket that was tied to a rope. The house was on the very edge of the city, and so St. Paul got away.

Sometimes on Sunday, you hear a reading, the second lesson from the Bible. If you notice, most of the time these lessons are letters of St. Paul that he wrote back to the places where he had preached about Our Lord. Tomorrow, get out your geography map and take a look at the Mediterranean Sea and find all the places where St. Paul preached. (Not now! Tomorrow, I said!) You will find places like Corinth, Ephesus, Colossae, Thessalonica—and on they go! He wrote to these people, just like our bishop sometimes writes letters to us, and the priest reads them in church on a Sunday.

And now, to tell you the greatest thing about St. Paul!

He got to see heaven! Yes, he did, and you might think that he would have come back and have given us an exact picture of what heaven looked like—you know, golden streets and all that. But it was so beautiful that St. Paul couldn't even talk—or write about it. So, here is the way he put it (your Bible has this): *Eye has not seen, nor ear heard, nor has it entered into the mind of man to conceive the things God has prepared for those who love him.*

I guess that by this time, you have been wondering why St. Paul used the word "*not*" so much, like when he says, *Eye has NOT seen, NOR has ear heard*. Actually, heaven is so beautiful that St. Paul did not know what to say. But really, he is telling you to build up all the marvelous things that your eyes ever saw, and when you have your own picture of the prettiest of everything, well, St. Paul still says, *"Go on back and read what I wrote. Your eye has not yet seen."* And then he goes on to say that you can put together all the loveliest songs that you ever heard, and that his answer will still be waiting for you in print: *Ear has not heard.*

And, finally, this great missionary tells you that you may go on building your finest castles in Spain and that you may pile on top of each other the most beautiful places you would ever like to see, and when all the building is finished, St. Paul will charmingly tell you to go back and read what he wrote: *It has not yet even entered into your mind the things that God has prepared for those who love him.*

Well, that's about it, young ones. And now, let's say a *Hail Mary* for all the priests and nuns, religious sisters and brothers and their helpers who are trying to be other St. Pauls—a long way from home.

Now go to sleep. But say that *Hail Mary* first!

3
SAINT KATERI TEKAKWITHA
- The Lily of the Mohawks -

A lot of you boys and girls know about the first people to settle in North America. They have been called by different names: Indigenous, Native Americans, Indians, and First Nations. One of them was a girl born into the Mohawk tribe of the Iroquois nation in 1656. Her name was Kateri Tekakwitha, and she would become the first-ever Native American saint.

Let's rewind to her mom, whose name may have been called Tagaskouita (say that three times fast). Kateri's mom was part of the Algonquin tribe, and she grew up in a village east of Montreal, surrounded by French missionaries. Due to the prayers and influence of the French Jesuit priests close to her, Tagaskouita decided to convert to Catholicism. At that time, her tribe, the Algonquins, was at war with the Mohawks.

One day, without warning, Mohawk warriors raided Tagaskouita's village, captured her, and carried her off to their homeland. Suddenly, she was a prisoner—ripped away from her family and home, all she had ever known—and taken on a long, dangerous journey south: 245 miles through wilderness, without even a single gas station for snacks.

Eventually, Tagaskouita was brought to a village called Ossernenon (say that four times fast) in present-day Auriesville, New York. She had no idea what was going to happen to her. In this foreign place among complete strangers, Tagaskouita was received into the Mohawk Turtle clan, which sometimes assimilated captives, in order to make up for their shrinking population due to war and disease.

Tagaskouita soon learned that she had to hide her faith. You see, the Mohawks disliked the "Blackrobes," as they called Catholic priests, along with the religion that came with them. The village of Ossernenon was even the site of the martyrdom of three Jesuit missionaries (Isaac Jogues, René Goupil, and Jean de Lalande) in the 1640s. Tagaskouita found only one Catholic friend named Anastasia Tegonhatsihonga, and they had to pray in secret. Remember that name. . . Anastasia.

A chief of the Mohawks ended up taking Tagaskouita as his wife, and in 1656, she gave birth to a little girl. And that is how Kateri Tekakwitha came into this world. When Kateri was old enough, Tagaskouita secretly taught little Kateri how to say prayers in her native language, such as the Our Father and the Hail Mary, which gave shape and direction to Kateri's destiny.

Mohawks didn't give their youngsters final names until they were seven or eight, so as a baby, Kateri was named Ioragode, which means "sunshine." Very appropriate, because her soul would shine, even when life got very, very dark.

And it did. When she was four, a smallpox outbreak swept through their village. Her mom, dad, and baby brother all passed away. Kateri survived—but her face was scarred, and the illness made her eyes so sensitive to light that if she went outside, she had to wear a blue blanket on her head like a one-girl mobile tent.

Poor Kateri! But that is where God comes in. You see, God is the best parent ever and He LOVES His children. He is called God the Father because He is everyone's Father. And He sends Mother Mary, as a comfort, too. So, God the Father and the Blessed Mother "stepped in" and parented Kateri in a very special way to make up for her terrible loss. When God's children are suffering and carrying a heavy cross, and their hearts are open, He fills them up on the inside with His Love, His Light, His Mother, and His Kingdom.

Jesus is one with God, and remember that Jesus said:

> "Let the children come to me, and do not prevent them; for the kingdom of heaven belongs to such as these." (Matthew 19:14)

That means that it's yours, too, dear child! Jesus is also saying that the Kingdom of Heaven belongs to you. You can ask Him now to invite the Kingdom of God to live inside of you! [Please take a moment now to do this.]

So, when Kateri's eyesight was damaged, her spiritual vision became clearer. The "Our Father" and "Hail Mary" prayers echoed in her soul, helping her to experience the bright light of God communicating to her through different thoughts and movements of the heart. It was through the cross that Kateri's soul started to grow very bright—like her very first name.

Kateri's uncle, the new clan chief, adopted her—though he didn't exactly win any "World's Best Uncle" mugs. And his wife and sister, who were Kateri's two aunts, helped take care of her. When Kateri turned seven or eight, she received her final Mohawk name— one that according to their custom, describes the child in some way. She went from being Ioragode, or *sunshine*, to *Te Ka Kwitha*, which means, "She who moves forward, moving something in front of her." So, either Tekakwitha was known for putting things in order—or for bumping into stuff. Since she couldn't see well and probably had to feel her way around, I'm guessing that her bumping into things gave her that name. If you're scratching your head, wondering how she also got the name Kateri. Well, just hold your horses. I'll get to that before you have to go to bed.

At first, little Kateri felt frustrated over having to spend most of her time staying inside her longhouse—which was exactly that, by the way: a house so long that it could shelter several families. When Kateri reflected on her situation later, she saw her sheltered life as a good thing because in a way, God was protecting her eyes from bad things—kind of like when your parents say, "You're not watching that movie until you're 30." After all, the Mohawks were warriors who tortured prisoners of war, and they didn't have any pure and chaste examples to look up to, like Joseph and Mary. Kateri never wanted to see anyone hurt, and she also wasn't interested in going to the dances or games that the Mohawks enjoyed. Instead, she stayed inside and probably bumped into furniture.

Kateri Tekakwitha lived in a time of European colonialism, which was really hard on the Native Americans, and not only that, the Algonquin and Iroquois nations weren't exactly besties. We're talking more "war dance" than "dance party." But in contrast to the world's turmoil and upset, Kateri brought peace and goodness to everyone around her; she was meek, patient, hard-working, honest, sweet, and innocent.

As Kateri's eyesight improved, she basically turned into a one-girl craft store. She could now do all the amazing things Indigenous women did—including making bead collars so beautiful they could've been sold at Etsy's top tier. That is, if Etsy had existed in the 1600s. She also made shell beads called wampum, which were basically the original version of Venmo, except a lot shinier and way easier to misplace.

And that's not all. Kateri could turn eel skin and tree bark into ribbons—yes, ribbons. Meanwhile, most of us can barely untangle our earbuds. She wove mats for the floor, bedding to sleep on, and even buckets for drawing water. Using nature and Native American genius, she ground corn like a pro, set up drying racks (Martha Stewart has no idea how to do that), and served meals. Eventually, her eyes got so good that her artistry shone in her belts of colorful patterns, made of moosehide and porcupine quills, which became people's favorites. Wait... porcupine quills, really? Those things are basically nature's tiny swords.

The Indigenous peoples really knew how to live off the land and make good use of everything that nature provided them. Nowadays, we have no idea how to weave a watertight basket out of leaves, and we don't even know where bananas come from.

When Kateri was 11, the Mohawks and the French colonists finally made peace. As a result, Kateri's uncle, the chief, was asked to host three Jesuit priests for three days. He did so reluctantly, and asked Kateri to take care of them. Kateri ended up being greatly impressed by these French Jesuits who spoke Iroquois and were probably the first white Christians she had ever seen. They admired her gentleness, attentiveness, and wholesomeness, and she liked their peaceful, kind ways and how often they prayed. They spoke to her about Jesus Christ, and this caused the sunshine of God in her heart grew even bigger.

Like every Native American girl, Kateri was expected to marry. There was no such thing as a young woman deciding to remain single—so her fate wasn't her own. When she was thirteen, her relatives decided she was ready. Kateri complained that she was too young. Her family listened to her for a while, but then decided they had found the right man. According to the ways of the Mohawks, if a young man came into a girl's family longhouse at night and sat next to her, it meant he was taking her as his wife.

One night, Kateri received a huge shock. A young man entered her longhouse and sat down next to her. So, what did she do? Kateri blushed, stood up, and ran into the woods like it was a dating show elimination. She was consumed by a desire to remain a virgin and never marry.

Now it was her relatives' turn to be shocked. How could a young woman—a Mohawk girl, reject marriage? After that, Kateri's relatives did not treat her well—more like a slave, to pressure her into changing her mind. But Kateri's heart was already given to God. Even though she didn't fully know who Jesus was yet, the sunshine of God was so bright in her soul that she somehow knew she belonged to Him alone.

At the age of 18, everything changed. A French Jesuit missionary named Fr. Jacques de Lamberville came to her village. Her uncle didn't like this "Blackrobe," nor his strange new religion, nor his new chapel nearby, but he tolerated his presence. Kateri walked every day to the chapel in order to listen to the daily prayers and teachings that Fr. Lamberville gave, but she didn't dare share with anyone her growing desire to become a Catholic.

One day, the Lord gave Kateri the perfect opportunity to express her secret wish. It happened because she had wounded her foot (God's perfect timing), so she couldn't gather corn in the fields like the other women. Fr. de Lamberville started making his rounds to instruct villagers in the faith, and when he stopped by her longhouse, Kateri couldn't hide her joy. She was finally able to share her biggest secret! Exploding like someone winning a Bible Bee, she exclaimed, "I want to be baptized!" Her goodness, simplicity, and excitement convinced Fr. de Lamberville to give her catechism lessons over the next two years, and on Easter Sunday in 1676, Kateri Tekakwitha was baptized at age twenty. That is when she took the name "Kateri," the Iroquois version of St. Catherine.

After her baptism, life became much harder for Kateri. Many Mohawks believed that Christianity had brought disease and death to their people. Her uncle was furious and worried that other young people would follow her example. He had already lost his oldest daughter, who had left to live with her husband in a Catholic mission called Sault St. Louis, far away from home.

Because Sunday is the Lord's Day of prayer and rest, Kateri didn't work in the fields, like the others. Instead, she went to Sunday Mass and prayed for most of each day, kneeling on the cold chapel floor for hours. Her family accused her of being lazy, and refused to feed her. But they couldn't shake her firmness, so on Sundays, she fasted without food. When Kateri would walk a straight path to the chapel, drunk people and children, encouraged by her relatives, would throw stones at her and shout, "The Christian!" as if that was something bad. So, she had to start walking in windy, roundabout ways to get there. Kateri's aunt even spread a lie about her, saying she did very inappropriate things with her uncle. It was heartbreaking. Kateri was totally innocent and pure, carrying a heavy cross that came not from enemies, but from the very people who should've had her back. But that's Kateri for you—graceful under fire (and rocks), faithful through it all.

One day, while Kateri was just minding her own business in her longhouse—probably doing something peaceful like praying, weaving, or reorganizing porcupine quills by color, a young man burst in suddenly, filled with rage and holding a hatchet in his hand, which he raised over his head. Maybe he just wanted to frighten her, but Kateri bowed her head without showing any emotion. Her bravery astonished the young Mohawk so much that he ran away, as if terrified by a ghost. Who do you think that invisible power was who protected her?

Kateri was learning the power of the cross. Her life of hardships had a purpose, she realized—even the scars on her face had great meaning. Her crosses were making her become more like Jesus. When she united, in her mind, her hardships with Jesus' sufferings on the Cross, this gave her the incredible power to help Him heal and save souls.

But even saints-in-the-making are human. She was tired of being treated like an enemy for loving God and just wanted to live somewhere she could practice her Catholic faith in peace without dodging rocks, rumors, or raging relatives. So, she started praying for this. It wasn't going to be easy because her uncle, the chief, had control over her and kept an eye on her like a hawk in a bad mood. Kateri was scared of him.

But God had a plan, like He always does. The Lord inspired a desire in Kateri's half-sister's heart to have Kateri brought to their mission of Sault St. Louis. She asked her husband if he would go find Kateri. Amazingly, he bravely and selflessly agreed to the treacherous mission. He would be trekking through untamed wilderness for months with no guarantee of ever returning. Yet he and his wife said yes to this inspiration that came from God on High, Who out of love for Kateri, was answering her prayer. With tearful goodbye's, the husband set out. Disguised as a beaver-skin trader doing business with the English, he travelled for two long months with a Christian Huron Indian and others, avoiding moose traffic and sharing the Good News of Jesus Christ with various Iroquois villages along the way. Finally, he found Kateri, and he told her of their plan. She was overjoyed!

In July of 1677, Kateri packed a blanket and nothing more because she didn't want to be accused of stealing anything, and when her uncle was away (pro tip), she left the village with her two escorts, the husband and the Huron. When the chief came home and realized she was gone, he loaded three musket balls into his gun and stormed off in hot pursuit, like an angry dad who just found out someone changed the Netflix password.

The travelers expected a chase, so when they stopped to rest, Kateri hid in the bushes (pro tip #2). Sure enough, here came the chief—moving like the wind, filled with fury. But her escorts stayed cool, acted casual, chatted with him like it was just another Tuesday, pretended like they were just there for the pelts. Strangely, the chief just. . . left. No threats, no yelling, no musket fireworks. Just an about face, a miraculous "Chief-Exit-Stage-Left."

Kateri was stunned. This was not the uncle she knew. She believed that God had again graced her with divine protection. Kateri and her two native guides continued to travel for over two months through woods, rivers, and swamps, finally reaching the Catholic mission of St. Francis Xavier at Sault Saint-Luis, near Montreal, in October of 1677. Kateri arrived physically weakened by the difficult journey, but happy. One can only imagine everyone's joy and relief.

It was there on the banks of the St. Lawrence River that Kateri Tekakwitha quickly made a name for herself as a faithful disciple of Christ, gaining the respect of all in the mission village. She lived in a longhouse with her half-sister and brother-in-law. And guess who was at the mission? Anastasia Tegonhatsihonga—her mom's old friend from forever ago, the only one she had prayed with in secret. Can you imagine the emotions? Kateri hadn't seen anyone from her mom's life since she was four years old, when memories are like shadows. Anastasia became her mentor, her guide, and her connection to the past.

On Christmas Day, only two months after Kateri had arrived, she received her First Communion. Jesus Christ in the Holy Eucharist filled her heart with such thanksgiving that she wantexd more prayer and more crosses. She started getting up for a 4 a.m. Mass (not even alarm clocks do that), then attended a *second* Mass at sunrise. During the day, she would commune with Jesus at the foot of the chapel altar or circle the cornfields with prayer—even in the bitterly cold winter of 1679. The Hail Marys that Kateri remembered saying as a little girl with her mother became a full Rosary that she recited many times a day. When out in the woods, she carved a cross on a tree, made crosses with sticks, and walked in a pattern forming a cross, with nature as her chapel. In the evening, Kateri would always return again to the indoor chapel, kneel on the cold floor, and not leave until late at night. Kateri seemed entirely unaware of what was going on around her when she prayed. In these intimate moments, when the sunshine in her heart merged with the light of divine love, she reached great heights of radiant union with God.

Kateri was loved by everyone, both French and Indian. The kids at the mission wanted her company so much that the catechism classes were moved to her longhouse to keep them happy. Surrounding her times of prayer, she worked hard, carving spoons and bowls, scraping fur (ew), cooking meals, collecting branches, and no doubt making rosary beads out of anything that wasn't nailed down. The community felt it was their sacred duty as Native Americans and Christians to give food and shelter to anyone who asked. The mission welcomed 800 guests in a single year, which is kind of a lot when you're mainly living off corn.

At one point, Kateri's mentor Anastasia and her best friend at the mission, Marie-Therèse Tegaiaguenta, surprised her—each on their own—insisting that she get married because they worried that no one would be there to take care of her as she got older. Kateri ran to her new spiritual Father, the Jesuit priest, Pierre Cholonec, who also wanted her well taken care of, but cared more that she follow the will of God. "Pray about it for three days," he advised her.

Kateri came back just a half hour later and said, "It is settled; it is not a question for deliberation. My decision has long since been made. No, my Father, I can have no other spouse but Jesus Christ."

Kateri fell so in love with her Spouse that she wanted to be completely united with Him on His Cross. The more crosses she carried, the brighter God's sunshine in her soul, and the more graces she could obtain, especially for the salvation and forgiveness of her family. She would deny herself comforts and perform many penances, like putting thorns on her sleeping mat, or piercing her skin, which was a Mohawk practice. She once burned her foot with a hot branding iron, not unlike the Mohawks branded their slaves, because she wanted to be a slave for Christ. Please, kiddos, do not try this at home—or anywhere, and definitely don't try this on your sister or brother. When Fr. Cholonec encouraged Kateri to take better care of herself, she laughed and continued with her "acts of love." "I will willingly abandon this miserable body to hunger and suffering," she said, "provided that my soul may have its ordinary nourishment."

In wintertime, the Indigenous Catholics would leave the mission community to hunt for meat. But in the cold winter of 1679, despite Fr. Cholonec's encouragement otherwise, Kateri preferred to stay at the mission where the only available food was corn. This is how much she wanted to be near Jesus in the Eucharist and away from distractions. Her health suffered, but, as usual, she never complained or showed the slightest signs of impatience.

After Kateri turned 24, her health began to fade. When a new priest, Fr. Chauchetière, arrived at the mission, she was already too sick to leave her bed. The father was so inspired by her witness, words and radiant faith, at a time when his own was wavering, that he considered her his great spiritual mentor. In just six weeks of regular visits, she had completely restored his priesthood.

As Holy Week approached, the community saw that their beloved sunshine was at the point of dying. The mission wanted to be near her. Around 3 p.m. on Holy Wednesday, April 17, 1680, the chapel bell was rung, and all the natives gathered in Kateri's longhouse, kneeling in prayer, accompanied by the priests, Fathers Chauchetière and Cholenec. Surrounded by love and prayer, and held in the arms of Marie-Therèse, she said her last words: "Iesos! Wari!" which means "Jesus! Mary!" And she fell into what looked like a peaceful sleep. Then, to everyone's astonishment, something miraculous happened...

This is how Fr. Cholenec described what he saw: "Her face suddenly changed and became, in a moment, so beautiful, smiling and white. Her face had an appearance of a rosy color, which she had never had, and her features were not the same. I saw this immediately, because I was praying beside her, and I cried out in my astonishment. Her face had been so scarred with smallpox from the age of four years old, and her infirmities and mortification contributed to ruin her even more. And before her death, she had taken a darker complexion. Her face appeared more beautiful than when she had been alive... Kateri Tekakwitha died as she had lived. That is to say, as a saint."

The white lily is a Christian symbol for purity of heart, chastity, and inner beauty. Because of the way Kateri had lived, she would come to be known as the Lily of the Mohawks, a sign for the whole world. In the weeks after her death, three people experienced apparitions of Kateri. According to their own testimony, Kateri appeared to Fr. Claude Chauchetière for two hours, surrounded in glory, and she knocked on Marie-Thérèse's wall, waking her up to say, "I am on my way to heaven." . . . "Go tell the father. . ."

When Anastasia was praying in the longhouse and had just rested her head on her mat to sleep, Kateri woke her up and said, "Mother, arise." Without any fear, Anastasia sat up and saw Kateri standing near her, glowing in brilliant light. Half of her body was hidden up to her waist in this radiance, and the other half was visible and glowing like the sun. Kateri was carrying in her hand a wooden cross shining more brightly than all the rest. Nothing Anastasia had ever seen was more beautiful than that cross. "Mother," Kateri called out, "Look at this cross. Oh! How beautiful it is! It has been my whole happiness during my life, and I advise you to also make it yours."

Now go to sleep and dream of sunshine.

4

SAINT PATRICK

- The Man Who Won Ireland for Our Lord -

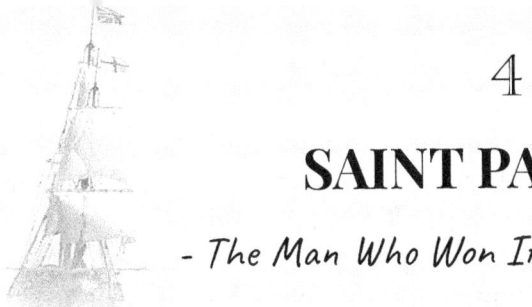

Well, youngsters, first of all, let's get the heartbreak over and done with! St. Patrick was not an Irishman. No sir! He was born a good many miles from Ireland—that Ireland which he would love and work for all his life. You see, there is this Irish Sea between Ireland and England, and St. Patrick was born on the English side of it, maybe in Scotland, maybe in England, maybe even on the coast of France. Nobody knows just where.

Anyway, we have him born now; so let's begin.

They did not have religion education classes in those days, so Patrick was nothing special as a young Christian. He just sort of went through the motions, never really facing up to God. In fact, he was 16 years old before he realized that God was knocking at his door. And by that time, he was a slave!

What happened was this. The people in Ireland did not know about Our Lord yet, so they were pretty bad. We would call them pagans, because they adored just about anything that came down the pike. Pike means a street. Now, these Irish pagans had a habit of getting into their ships and sailing around and beating up on different towns. On this one trip, they came to the place where Patrick lived. They licked that town, too, and put Patrick into one of their ships and made him their slave. Then they all went back to Ireland.

When they got back home, they gave Patrick the job of watching their sheep on the side of a mountain called Slemish, and that is where God began to nudge our hero. Day after day, Patrick watched the sheep, but, after all, he could not talk to them, much less pray to them and love them, so he gradually began to lift his eyes and his heart to the God of his childhood. And I am sure that, at that moment, everything in Ireland found itself a little greener. And perhaps a bit more pure. Patrick did not know it, but he was on his way to bringing Ireland to the feet of our Lord.

(We might say right here that this is why lots of moms and dads like to make a retreat once a year. Like St. Patrick, they find God all over again there in the silence and in the prayer. And they find *themselves* all over again, too.)

But back to St. Patrick!

By this time, Our Lord knew that Patrick was loving Him pretty well, so he decided the moment had come for our future saint to begin his study for the priesthood.

Patrick was already 22 years old. It was the year 410. The night was peaceful, and suddenly there were mysterious voices telling Patrick to leave at once for the seashore. That meant he must walk over 200 miles, with his master's soldiers and dogs following him and tracking him. But the road to the priesthood would never be an easy one. Patrick hitched up his belt and got going.

Walking, running, hiding, begging for food, sleeping along the hedges, Patrick made it. The seashore at last! And surely enough, there was a ship getting up sail. But now Patrick had more trouble. No money! The sailors told him he could not ride without paying, but our saint just went back to his prayers, and the next thing he knew, the captain told him to get aboard the ship anyway. And talk about hoping in God! Patrick did not even know where the ship was going! The *voices* had simply told him he was going back to his family. St. Patrick simple writes: "I trusted God completely."

Well, the ship went all over the place, and Patrick gave the sailors quite a run for their money. At first, they laughed at him because of his belief in Our Lord and Our Lady, but whenever they stopped on land and were starving in lonely places, they would always ask Patrick to pray, and sure enough some food would turn up. They were awfully glad he was along. Once they brought him some honey, and it looked just fine to Patrick, but then they told him it must be eaten in honor of the pagan gods. Patrick just looked at them and put down the honey. "Thanks be to God," he said years later, "I tasted none of it."

Maybe that is where youngsters got the beautiful old custom of giving up candy during Lent, and it really fits right in, because St. Patrick's feast day, March 17, is smack-dab in the middle of Lent.

But now and at long last, a little human happiness came into our saint's life. One fine morning as he walked along, the road began to look familiar, the hills seemed to be the hills of home, and Patrick gathered his rags about him and ran, ran into the heart of his own family. What a joyful reunion it was. And so for a while, Patrick caught his breath and stretched his legs around the old hometown; but you can be sure that the Good Lord had not gone to all that trouble with Patrick just to have him sit around the house and get fat. Nor had Patrick forgotten those days and nights on the mountain, when he had been so close to his God; nor had he forgotten those voices. And now the voices began to whisper to him again. They were Irish voices, and they cried softly to him: "We beseech thee, holy youth, to come and walk among us once more."

St. Patrick looked around him, startled. What could he do? What must he do? He wanted to be close to Our Lord in the priesthood, and he knew, too, that he could not go back and work for Ireland's conversion to Catholicism unless he went back as a priest. But he knew nothing of the things that a priest must know. And do you know what he did? He just buckled down to study at the age of 23 and went to schools in France for years until he was ordained a priest. Then, 15 years after he had left Ireland, he was made a bishop by St. Germanus. This holy man pointed to the west, to

Ireland, and told Patrick to go and get it for Christ. Patrick went with a song in his heart.

So back to the green hills of Ireland he went. But remember—in the eyes of the Irish he was no bishop, but just a runaway slave. Well, the Irish had a lot to learn, for this was a new Patrick now, with the burning love of our Lord in his heart and all the power of the priesthood at his fingertips. He was buying no nonsense from anyone. He did not fool around with the small towns. He was a bishop, representing the whole Christian Church in Ireland, and he wanted to meet, head-on, the highest Irish chief. That chief would be the High King Leary, the place would be Tara, the mountain would be Slane, and the day would be Easter Sunday.

Now, the pagan Irish priests were called Druids, and you can be sure they were not very happy to see Patrick coming down the pike. (There's that pike again!) These Druids were supposed to be magicians, and both the king and the people were pretty scared of them. The Druids were out to get St. Patrick. They picked the wrong man. St. Patrick got them.

But back to Easter morning. The law was that nobody was to light a fire in the Easter dawn until after the High King Leary lighted his own pagan fire there at Tara. Well, St. Patrick had his own idea of Easter dawn, the resurrection hour of his Master, and so he lit up one beauty of a fire on top of Slane Mountain, while Leary was still looking around for a match (or something!) Well, gosh golly, up the hill of Slane came thundering King Leary and his pagan lads, with the Druids bringing up a safe rear. But Patrick stood his ground, and the great saint preached to them all about Our Lord, and what Easter morning really meant.

The Druids listened and watched. They knew they had better do something fast, if they wanted to go on druiding, so they challenged St. Patrick to a few rounds of magic. They couldn't have made a worse choice. St. Patrick called upon the Almighty, and the next thing you know, the chief Druid was sailing through the air and landed on his head where his feet should have been. He lay

there pretty quiet, and the men of Ireland knelt in obedience to Patrick. It was the beginning.

And then for 30 years, St. Patrick went up and down the length and width of Ireland, bringing the faith to them all. You might put his whole life's idea this way: "Stay very close to God, and work, work, work for Him." He baptized hundreds of thousands of people, he built 700 churches, he ordained 5,000 Irish priests, and consecrated 370 bishops. He came to Ireland to begin his work in the year 432, and just 10 years later, he had the whole Catholic picture set up and nailed down, with a city called Armagh as the headquarters of the chief bishop: himself.

The way that St. Patrick did all this was thrilling. It must have been glorious to be with him. He had the strangest army you ever saw. They were not soldiers. Among them there were young boys studying to be priests, as they went with the saint from town to town; there were carpenters and blacksmiths; there were ironworkers and bronzeworkers; there were ladies who made altar cloths and did embroidery work; there were cooks and bakers and shoemakers—and at the head of it all was Patrick.

They would come thundering into a town on horseback, in chariots, in wagons; St. Patrick would step down and have a heart-to-heart talk with the chief of the place, letting him know that the religion of Our Lord had come to him, that all Ireland was going Catholic, that the faith of Christ was in the air, and that the boys would start building the new church at 3 o'clock that afternoon. And it really went that way. There was no persecution of the Church. Oh, the Druids would try to kill Patrick now and then, but it was risky work, what with all the big Irish Christian lads about the place. The Druids had died at Tara. The rest was a drawn-out burial ceremony.

So, the churches sprang up all over Ireland. Up would ride the army of Patrick; the carpenters and the blacksmiths, the ironworkers and the bronzeworkers unloaded their tools, and everybody built that church with Patrick in the lead. The altars were made, and the ladies put their beautiful

Irish linen upon them. Nails were hammered out; hinges were wrought; a Tabernacle took shape beneath the hands of men who worked in bronze. Then Patrick would call aside one of the young priests he had trained and ordained along the road.

"Take care of them, lad."

And off would go this little army of God to the next town, leaving new church and new priest behind them, and let's see a modern assembly line beat that!

It all seems as fresh as a spring morning, and yet, dear children, all this happened 1500 years ago. Yes, the great Patrick lit his Easter fire on the hill of Slane just 400 years after the first Easter dawn.

But finally, as had to be, there came the day when our great saint had to slow down his tireless riding for Christ. Dear heavens, what one man had done! It makes us wonder what we can do for Our Lord in the life ahead of us. Yes, St. Patrick was old now, and tired, but not too tired to climb the towering Mount Aigli, and fast there for 40 days and 40 nights, praying for his people, and at last rising up to bless them and their children forever.

Dear, wonderful saint! He used up all his life for God, and God was his strong right arm. Patrick wanted and needed nothing else.

We pause a final moment and go back to the dark hour when Dichu, a great Irish pagan chief, came storming down to the beach to attack Patrick on the very day he landed as Bishop Patrick, come back to win Ireland for Christ.

What happened was this, as one old writer says: "When Dichu looked at the face of Patrick, he loved him."

So do we all. It is that simple.

Now go to sleep, me darlins!

5

SERVANT OF GOD JULIA GREELEY

- God's Secret Night Angel -

Well, youngsters, pull up the covers. Tonight we're going to talk about a lady who was small in this world but very big in God's eyes. Her name is Julia Greeley, and she didn't have it easy—not one bit.

She was born a slave, and no one ever told her the date of her birthday. So there were no candles, no cake, no kid party—no nothin'. When she was little, a whip meant for her mother struck Julia instead and blinded her right eye, leaving it drooping. That was the world she was born into—one where children had to grow up too fast and there wasn't much to celebrate. But slavery ended in 1865 through the Emancipation Ordinance of Missouri, and Julia was free.

Around 1879 she moved to Denver, Colorado, and worked as a household servant for the Gilpins. This is an important piece of her story because Mrs. Gilpin shared with Julia a gift better than all the treasure in the world. No… not a Lamborghini (mothers, explain why that was impossible). She shared the Catholic faith—and that gift became the joy of Julia's whole life. The two women, loving God together, became fast friends.

But Mr. Gilpin didn't like this much at all. He had once been governor of Colorado and got into a pile of trouble by promising money he didn't have during the Civil War. People were angry at him, and he was a really grumpy guy. He and his wife quarreled and quarreled. One day, to hurt his wife, he fired Julia. Worse, he spread ugly stories about her—especially about the color of her skin.

Those lies made it nearly impossible for Julia to find work in Denver. She was forced to travel all over the United States to support herself for five whole years, working as a domestic worker or day laborer, unable to write anything or read much, since she'd never been allowed to go to school. Meanwhile, Mr. Gilpin dragged his wife into court to get a divorce and filed twenty-four complaints—one of them called Julia "lewd and unprincipled." Pretty darn mean.

These accusations caused people to judge Julia harshly, but she never complained. In the end, the court saw through the lies and cleared her good name. Some people thought that Julia should ask for money from Mr. Gilpin to make up for all the pain he caused her, but she would say to that, "They've given me more than money—they gave me my faith." Julia was just that way. People could throw false accusations, prejudice, and gossip at her. They could take away jobs and a good reputation from her, but nobody could steal her peace or the treasure she had found in God.

Now, in those days, Black parishioners were expected to sit apart from white parishioners, and people sometimes rented pew space. Julia rented a pew up front on the left at Sacred Heart Church, and a few proud and prejudiced ladies didn't like that at all. Julia was black, poor, wore second-hand clothes, limped from years of hard work, and had that half-closed eye. They muttered that she didn't belong up front, looking like she did. Hearing about this, Julia humbly told her pastor that she could go to another Mass, but he was having none of it. "Julia," he replied, "you're going to keep your regular seat and come to high Mass, like you always do, because I know you want to. Julia can sit any place in this church she wants to."

Julia kept going to that church—day after day—kneeling, folding her hands, and lifting her heart to God. She took up fasting for the Lord and would say, "The Eucharist is my breakfast." In 1901 she became a Third Order Franciscan and chose the saint name Elizabeth, after the princess-saint, Elizabeth of Hungary, who spent her life serving the poor—sometimes in secret.

Julia found rest in Jesus' Sacred Heart, and no doubt she needed it because she was always up late serving Him. You see, although Julia never had much money of her own, she somehow managed to help others who had even less by trusting in God's providence. Julia would pull a little red wagon through the streets of Denver after dark, even when her limp, arthritic joints and old bones began to slow her steps. Overnight, families who were struggling—widows, children, men out of work—would find food, clothing, and firewood at their doors.

Julia chose the nighttime on purpose. She knew that poverty could make people feel ashamed. She wanted no one to see her arrive, no one to feel embarrassed by her help. She would leave her bundled gifts silently and secretly. One winter night, Julia carried a sack of potatoes to a house and worried they might freeze before the family discovered them. So she sent a boy to knock and then run. "Don't you dare say Old Julia sent you!" she told him firmly. Another time, when young girls in her parish felt too embarrassed to come to youth events because they couldn't afford nice dresses, Julia took a walk to the rich part of town. She knocked on the front doors of wealthy families, asking them to buy new dresses for their daughters so that she could pass their gently used dresses on to "her girls." This arrangement soon became an expected ritual, since Julia convinced them that their daughters needed new dresses on a regular basis.

Julia's red wagon didn't just carry food and clothing; it carried joy. Her laugh was contagious—big, hearty, and warm. The little squirts of Denver adored her. When it came time for them to have a confirmation sponsor, "Aunt Julia" was a favorite. Why? She told stories that made eyes go wide, sang and danced right along with them, made them laugh, and gathered them up for trolley rides and picnics.

Julia had a special love for firefighters. The Denver firemen risked their lives daily, and Julia worried about their souls. As a member of her parish's Sacred Heart League, she visited all of the

fire stations each month, walking in with pamphlets, Sacred Heart badges, and kind words. She wanted every firefighter to know Jesus's love and protection. She reminded them to be ready for sudden death and to trust in the Sacred Heart. The firemen, in turn, supported her. When young girls at her parish held a beauty-contest fundraiser, an elderly Julia entered herself to raise money for the poor. Everyone knew she wasn't there for a crown—she was there to collect votes. The firemen pitched in, buying 10 cent vote tickets by the hundreds, making sure that she won. In the end, Julia raised an astonishing $350—equal to $12,500 today—by selling 3,500 tickets!

Julia was once seen carrying a mattress on her back in a dark alley at night. She got clothes for grieving family who had nothing dignified to wear at their loved one's funeral, she cared for the sick when their caregivers were overburdened, and she often begged for whatever the poor might need. She even gave up her own grave so an elderly Black man could have a decent burial and not end up in a potter's field. Whether hauling her wagon through Denver's streets or climbing the steps of a neighbor's porch, her lips moved in prayer. If you didn't already guess it, her favorite devotion was to the Sacred Heart of Jesus, symbolized by the picture of Christ pointing to His Heart, burning with love for every soul.

Julia kept little Sacred Heart badges in her pockets and handed them out everywhere—children, poor folks, firefighters—so they'd remember: Jesus loves you with a Heart that never quits. She also loved Our Lady and prayed the Rosary every day. For Julia, work and prayer went together like a wagon and its wheels.

People noticed. They brought her their prayer needs, and she tucked them into what she called her "canoe" of prayers, rowing it straight to God's ear. In 1914, while working for Mrs. Agnes Urquhart, Julia learned that Agnes had been childless for ten years; her baby boy had died because he couldn't digest food, and the doctor had told her not to try to have children again. Julia said, "There will be a little white angel running around the house. I will pray and you will see." Sure enough, Agnes gave birth to a healthy girl named Marjorie—the little one you see in the only photograph we have of Julia, taken in 1916.

On June 7, 1918—the very Feast of the Sacred Heart—Julia set out, as usual, to walk to morning Mass. But she never made it. She collapsed in the street. A priest came to give her the last rites, and she was carried to St. Joseph's Hospital. Within hours, she was gone. Instead of walking into the Church of the Sacred Heart that day, she walked straight into Jesus' Sacred Heart—her "assured refuge at that last hour."

The Denver Post printed a simple notice regarding her funeral arrangements. Nearly one thousand mourners came. Even though the paper did not list the wake, when her viewing began at Loyola Chapel, crowds lined the streets. Hundreds of mourners of every age, status, and race flowed through the chapel for 5 straight hours to pay their respects, and news articles about Julia Greeley, Denver's "Angel of Charity," graced the local papers. Only after her death did many learn that an ex-slave with almost nothing to her name but a tiny room, a red wagon, and worn-out clothes, was the one who had rushed to their aid in their time of need.

A woman of true greatness had walked among them, chosen by Jesus to reflect to the world the love of His Sacred Heart.

Now go to sleep.

6

SAINT FRANCIS DE SALES

- The Sword Fighter with a Temper -

Well, youngsters, tonight we are going to talk to you about a good man who was especially known for holding back his temper. He really could hold it back. People used to call him the "meek one." (Meek means that we refuse to give in to our temper.) This man laughed when he heard about it. He told one of his friends: "For 40 years my temper has been so bad that I sometimes had to run into my room and hold my heart with both hands." But nobody ever knew it. He held back!

Anger is a pretty bad thing. Nobody wants you around at parties and things like that, if you always have to have your own way and lose your temper if you don't get it. Yelling and screaming do not prove that you are right. They prove that you are four-star knuckleheads.

So, let's take a look at St. Francis. He is the patron saint for many boys and men. A certain priest tells the following story: "When I went to the seminary to become a priest, I did not even know that there was more than one St. Francis. The priest who had charge of us asked me after which St. Francis I was named. I did not know, so he took one look at me and suggested that I take St. Francis de Sales, because he was the gentleman saint. Now, whatever do you think he meant by that?" (Mothers, explain!)

But about young Francis. He was bullheaded, all right, and he sure did land into trouble with it. His mother told him to stay out of the kitchen, one time, and to keep away from the pies she had baked. But not our little Francis. He sneaked in, like you do, and sank his teeth into a cherry pie. It was just out of the oven, and it was like fire in his mouth, so he just stood there, in his full eight-year growth, screaming for his mother, like you do. That's why I said you were knuckleheads. Don't you understand that your mother loves you? That's why she tells you what to do and what not to do.

Well, anyway, by that eternal miracle that lets children make their way through all the cyclones of childhood, Francis got up to his 11th birthday. There was one time when he thought he was not going to make it. Seems that he had a cousin in his schoolroom, and this cousin was always goofing off. One day, he really got into trouble and was about to be thrown out of school, but Francis got up and told the teacher that he, Francis, had really been the guilty one, and the teacher promptly took a stick and warmed Francis' seat. (Parent, explain, if you wish.) You can see right away that his bullheadedness was getting him into big trouble. He was even beginning to lie because of his bullheadedness, and a lie is never any good. He had wanted to be a big shot by taking his cousin's punishment, but that did not help his cousin grow up to be a truthful man. And it certainly did not help Francis, because he had to eat off the mantelpiece for a few days.

But the childhood days were about over now, and Our Lord began to nudge Francis. I guess you might call it a nudge or a push, or really, a grace. They all mean the same thing for our purpose here. It means that your brain sort of lights up, and you know you have time to make a visit to Our Lord in the Blessed Sacrament on your way home from school, and you do it; or you know that it is NOT your turn to do dishes, but your sister and brother have an awful lot of homework, and you take their place. (But on the next night, don't take it all back by saying: "I did the dishes last night!")

However, back to our story of Francis. Well, he had this grace from God, this little push toward real holiness, and he did not turn it down. At first, he thought he would be a great lawyer and fight for what was right in the law courts and please God that way. But Our Lord had some other ideas. He wanted Francis to be a priest!

Now, we have to understand that Francis was living at a time when things were different from right now. Nowadays, good Protestants and good Catholics are honestly trying to get together to see what can be done about having one flock and one shepherd. In those days they spent a lot of time fighting each other—swords and everything. The young man Francis sort of saw through things, and he said: "Catholics should learn to be angels before they become avenging angels." That word "avenging" is probably a little rough for the moppet crowd. It means that you had better be sure that you, yourself, are holy before you start telling somebody else how unholy he or she is.

Understand, now, and don't get me wrong . . . Francis was no sissy. In fact, he was possibly the best swordsman around Paris. And, with his temper, he had to prove his ability with the sword quite often. He did not kill anybody, just sort of nicked them to let them know who was boss.

But all this time, while Francis was studying law, Our Lord was sort of leading him along. One of the best things that happened to him was when Our Lord gave him the idea that he ought to start going to the same priest whenever he went to Confession. That way the priest could know him real well and help him make big decisions (especially about the priesthood). You should all keep that in mind your whole life. Try to go to the same priest for each Confession, so you can talk to him in case you have to make a big decision sometime. That way he knows what kind of person you are and can help you all the more. Of course, you don't have to.

Well, by now, you guessed it. Yes, Francis became Fr. Francis de Sales. Believe me, it wasn't easy. When he began to turn to thoughts of becoming a priest, his buddies at law school used to give him a pretty hard time when they saw him running out to Mass each morning. But now Francis was becoming bullheaded for God and for souls. He kept going to Mass each morning, even though the rule was that he (and all Catholics) could go to Holy Communion only a few times a year. (You are lucky, youngsters. Every morning you can receive Our Lord, your tongue, once more, becoming the cradle of Bethlehem.)

And don't be surprised if you find yourself in the same kind of trouble as Francis, when you're in grade school or further along the line. There will always be somebody there to laugh at you when you try to be good. Just be bullheaded for God like St. Francis was. Don't ever let anybody tell you that you have to be in his or her gang or go with him or her. Stand back and make up your own mind about that. The real flop is the boy or girl who is not bullheaded enough to tell somebody off when that person wants him to do something that he knows is wrong.

Just before he decided to be a priest, Francis had one good fight over all this. He was walking down a street one dark night, and a bunch of the college crowd, with masks on, jumped on him and cried out:

"Throw down your rosary!"

Well, they picked on the wrong person. Francis reached beneath his cloak, and I guess the college fellows thought he was going to pull out his rosary. Nothing doing. Francis pulled out his sword, backed into a corner, and fought them all until they sneaked away, realizing this man could fight as well as pray.

It is getting late now, and anyway, I just wanted to tell you about the young Francis, not about his later life. Yes, he became a priest, and after that, a bishop, a great bishop. With the right kind of bullheadedness, he fought for our Lord until his last breath. There is part of Switzerland and a city called Geneva where many strong and courageous Catholics are to be found. Their spiritual father is St. Francis de Sales.

St. Francis was a great saint, children, a great gentleman. And if there was anger in his heart, he turned it against the enemies of his dear Master, Our Lord. He turned his anger against their *sins*. His Master would never let him hate the *sinners*. Otherwise, he would not be SAINT Francis.

Now go to sleep!

7

SAINT EDMUND CAMPION

- The Martyr They Chased All Over England -

Well, young people, tonight we are going to talk about a part of the storybook of saints that will really get your ears wiggling. It will be all about a young man who had a great love for Our Lord, and he would do plenty for Him before they finally took his life.

But first let's get the stage all ready for him. You see, about 400 years ago, the king of England wanted to leave his wife and marry somebody else, and the pope would not let him. Well, between this king, Henry, and his daughter, Queen Elizabeth, the whole country of England was gradually turned away from being Catholic. It was not the people's fault. They were all mixed up and did not know where the new laws were coming from. They just sort of woke up one morning and were told that they had to turn their back on the pope and, pretty soon, on the Holy Mass, the Blessed Mother, the Confessional, and just about everything. And then they were told that the king was the new head of the Church for England. Not only that, but if you got caught going to Mass or hiding a priest in your house, you could get into real trouble—all the way from being fined and put in jail, to being hanged.

Now, by the time that our Edmund gets into the picture, the king was dead, and his daughter, Queen Elizabeth, was running the roost, and she was 20 times worse for the Catholics than her father was.

St. Campion took a pretty good look at the situation, and by the grace of God, decided to study to be a priest and help his own beloved people find their way back to God. In those days, a young man who wanted to study for the priesthood had to leave England and go away for his studies. Edmund went to Belgium and took up his studies at a place called Douai. He spent many years there and also in Rome, where he finally was all set to go back to England and work in the Catholic underground as a Jesuit priest.

Of course, at that time a priest could not simply sail over to England and say: "Look, I am a priest, and have to come back to save England!" Heavens no, they were all on the lookout for Edmund, so he made himself out to be a jewel seller, with Ralph, a Jesuit lay Brother, acting as his servant.

Edmund and Ralph came into the city of London one day and stood there on the banks of the River Thames, trusting God that their "contact man" would show up. By "contact man" we mean the person who would put them in touch with the faithful Catholics. Well, a wonderful man showed up. His name was Thomas Jay, and he and a lot of other young men had formed a club to help these priests. They had made a promise to do anything and everything to bring the true faith back to England. These young fellows must have really lived!

Actually, their meeting place was in the home of a rich young Catholic named George Gilbert, who was ready to use up all his money to help the priests get to the people to say holy Mass for them, give them Holy Communion, comfort them, and bring them the truth again. The funny thing about it was that Mr. Gilbert had rented this house from the chief of police of London, and while the chief and his men were looking all over town for them, the young Catholics and their priests were sitting in the chief's house, planning to make all of England Catholic again.

Oh, of course, the queen in her castle would call our friends "traitors." But don't you believe it. The real traitors were in the castle, and they were the ones who had betrayed the English people, stealing from them their faith, the sacraments, everything.

Now enters the miserable man who would hunt down Fr. Campion, betray him, sell him out, and finally set him on that last road to the gallows of Tyburn. This was the place where public hangings took place. This bad man's name was George Eliot, and he had often been in trouble with the police. When he heard how badly the queen and her helpers wanted to capture Fr. Campion, he figured that this was his chance to get in good with the higher-ups and maybe get a nice reward, too. He had a meeting with Leicester, a bad nobleman, and got a good description of Fr. Campion and began to track him down. He acted as though he was a very pious Catholic just dying to join the club of young Catholic men and have the privilege of meeting Fr. Campion. Actually, if he could just catch Edmund saying Holy Mass once, then he as good as had him on the road to Tyburn.

Meanwhile, our hero was not waiting around for George Eliot. He was traveling around the north of England, going from home to home, saying Mass and preaching to the people. As a rule, they were great houses, and people from all over that neighborhood would quietly come to receive the sacraments. One of the greatest things that Fr. Campion brought them was what we might call "direction." He told them the right road for Catholics to take in all this mix-up. He made it clear that they must not attend any church services of the new religion. (Things have changed little since then.) It was really tough on these good people. Many of them would lose all they owned. Many of them would also die at Tyburn; but they were heartsick for the truth and for God, and they went all the way for Him.

Lots of times, Edmund was almost caught by the soldiers of the queen, but for a long time, the people were able to hide him. Most of these big houses had a very secret little room called the "priest's hole," and the priest that said Mass would make a dash for it when the soldiers came. But when the soldiers came in too quickly, there was no time to get to the secret room, and the priest had to head for the forest and stay there, alone, hungry, hunted like an animal.

During all this time, Fr. Campion was in disguise. That is, he was not going around dressed in a black suit and white collar, as your priest does. He was still supposed to be the jewelry seller, and sometimes he did not look like much of anything, especially on one day when he was teaching catechism to a young servant girl in the garden of one of the great houses. Suddenly, the girl saw some soldiers riding up, and right in the middle of her catechism lesson she pushed Fr. Campion into a muddy fishpond just behind him. The soldiers came up and asked her if there was a traveling jewelry merchant around. They saw a very muddy young man spitting out water at the side of the pond, and he surely did not look like much of a salesman, so they rode on. Fr. Campion had to laugh as he thanked her for the dunking. It had saved his life, once more.

We said a while ago that Fr. Campion was tops in everything he did. Now, it was decided that he should write a little booklet explaining why the new religion was wrong. It was to be called the "Ten Reasons." Long before this, he had written a little book called "The Brag." Actually, the booklet was a sort of last will, and in it he told the world that he and his fellow priests had come back to England, not as traitors, but to live and die for the true religion. And now the "Ten Reasons" was being secretly printed so the people could read it and become stronger and stronger in the true faith. Sometimes when you read the old-time stories, England is called "Merry England." Well, you can easily see, by this time, that England was not very merry anymore. They had lost too much in the switch of religion that their rulers had forced.

But to get back to the "Ten Reasons". . . Oxford College graduation day was coming up, and, of course, that meant all kinds of speeches against the Catholics, the priests, and all they stood for. Well, one of the priests, Fr. Hartley, took a big pack of the "Ten Reasons" booklets, and on the night before graduation, he quietly made his way into the chapel at Oxford (where the speeches would

be given) and placed the booklets in every pew! You can imagine how Leicester, the queen's friend who hated Campion, blew his top the next day! Nobody had to tell him who had written the "Ten Reasons." He called in the miserable George Eliot and told him: "Get Campion!"

And off Eliot went to the north of England, asking around all the great Catholic houses his pious-sounding question: When was the great Fr. Campion coming to say Mass so that he, Eliot, might have the comforts of the true religion?

Well, you are starting to fall asleep, so I will hurry along to the moment when George Eliot finally caught St. Edmund. Father had been saying Holy Mass in the home of a wonderful, loyal, little old lady named Mrs. Yates. He had just finished the Mass when in came Eliot and his friends. The priests fooled them the first time and ran to a special little "priest's hole" that was very cleverly built right over the main gateway. Nobody could find them, and finally the searchers got tired and left.

After all, most of these searchers were neighbors of the Yates, and did not like this hunting. But Eliot started screaming that he would have them all put in jail if they did not go back and help him tear out every wall until they found the priests that he felt sure were somewhere in that house. They went back, and this time, the priests barely made it to their hiding place. Eliot was like a madman, and he and his men kept poking into walls.

Finally, it happened. They saw a bit of daylight shining through a crack in the false wall behind which the priests were hiding. Eliot called for tools; he broke open the wall, and the priests stood there. It was over. Eliot received his reward from Leicester. Fr. Campion received his from God. Which would you want?

Quietly, go to sleep, children.

8

SAINT JOAN OF ARC

- The Girl Who Won the Fight for France -

Everybody loves the story of Cinderella. It makes you feel good all over to think that this little girl, out of nowhere, all of a sudden, became the most beautiful person at that grand dance. Such a wonderful fairy story, with a prince and everything! But, as you know, Cinderella had to run home at midnight, or else everybody would turn into a pumpkin or something. Cinderella ran real fast and made it just in time.

Tonight let's talk about another young girl who came out of nowhere to become the most wonderful person in all the great country of France. (Of course, she had to come from somewhere, but I mean that nobody had heard much about her so far.) And, just like Cinderella, this young girl had a prince and there were palaces and everything. But the beautiful part is that this girl's story is no fairy tale at all. These things really happened.

Her name is Joan, and she is a saint. She is a saint because she went into the palace, not to dance but to do battle, to fight for Our Lord, and no matter how many times the bells would ring out at midnight, she would never run away from her battles for him. But let's tell her story.

It was springtime in the little village of Domremy, the home of St. Joan. Our story begins with her sitting beneath a tree, watching and taking care of her father's sheep. Then, suddenly, it happened! A voice whispered to her that she must go to the palace of the French king! Up she got and looked all around, but there was nobody there! She didn't know what to do and was getting real

scared, when just then the "voice" told her that he was St. Michael, and that not only did God want her to go to the palace, but she must also lead the French army into battle against the enemies of France. That just about floored Joan. After all, she was just a teenager and hardly knew which end of a sword to grab, much less how to fight with it or even lift it. They had real big swords then.

However, Joan had long ago learned to obey, and she knew that Our Lord was just as wise and strong as He was lovable and that He would take good care of her. "Who can beat God?" she figured. (We might say right here that sometimes it looks like some people are beating God, but they forget that God is also the umpire when the fight is over and that he decides who really won, anyway.)

In a short time, Joan began to find out what a lot of saints have found out—that, even though you are working for God, things can get pretty hard and miserable. That is because God trusts His saints to go right on working for Him while He (so to say) is somewhere else trying to put some sense into the heads of those who don't love Him and won't work for Him.

Anyway, Joan went to the palace of the king of France, who was called Charles the Seventh. At first, nobody paid her any attention. But, really, the king was pretty smart, and he had dressed up like any ordinary person and stood around in the middle of a big crowd, because he figured that if God had really sent Joan, then God would help her pick the king out of any crowd. And that is exactly what happened. Joan just walked past all those people and went right up to the king and said to him: "Your Majesty! It is God who commands that you go to battle against England and Burgundy!"

Of course, that did it. The king knew that Joan had never seen him before and that she was really the messenger of God, since God had directed her right to him.

So, Joan was made the leader of the whole French army. In those days people went to battle all wrapped up in metal to keep off the arrows. Joan had a suit made of real light metal. When everything was all ready, she mounted her horse at the head of that great army, raised the flag she had made, and off they went to the wars.

There was lots and lots of fighting, but God was on her side. So, they beat up everybody all the way to the beautiful city of Reims. And there, at last, in the great cathedral, while Joan watched with tears in her eyes, Charles was crowned king of all France.

But there was still some fighting to be done to make sure that France was really clear of all her enemies. Especially, there was some trouble around a town called Compiègne. Well, Joan and her soldiers rode out and pretty well cleaned up the enemy, but when they were going back into town, somebody made a mistake and slammed the big gate of the city wall before Joan could get inside. Joan tried to get away, but it was too late, and she was captured by a lot of soldiers whose leader was a man called John of Luxembourg. These people took her away and actually sold her to the English, who hated her because she had beaten them so badly at Orleans and lots of other places.

And then Joan found out all over again that Our Lord asks those whom He loves to suffer for Him and prove their love, as He did on the Cross. First of all, the French king would not even try to get her back from the English, after all she had done for him. He just let them take her to prison, where they put chains around her neck and hands and feet, and wouldn't even let her see a priest for Confession and Holy Communion.

The day came for her awful trial. Her enemies would not even give her a lawyer who might defend her. She answered all the questions simply and straight-out in court, so that any fair-minded person listening should have known that she had done nothing wrong. But then they began to ask her some real tricky questions, and the little girl from the springtime village of Domremy didn't quite know what they were talking about. She fell into their trap, gave a couple of wrong answers, and then they all jumped up and said that she had turned her back on God's religion and that she must be burned to death.

And that is the way that Joan died, dear children. She asked only for a cross that she might hold. Somebody tied two pieces of wood together, like a cross, and quickly gave it to her. (God bless him, whoever he was!) Then they tied her to a post and piled branches and logs around her feet and lit the fire. The flames came closer and closer, but Joan just held her little cross tight to her. And do you know what she kept on saying as the fire caught at her gown? She just kept on crying out softly: "Jesus . . . Jesus . . . Jesus!"

And, so, that is the way our great little saint died. And the waters of a river called the Seine shall ever be sacred, because they carried her ashes to the sea.

Oh, they straightened it all out later. The Holy Father, the pope, declared that the whole trial had been a horrible, unjust thing. And another Holy Father declared that she was a saint.

Maybe we think that it was pretty late in the day when people at last found out that she was really good and holy and even a saint. But St. Joan didn't worry about that. She just looked down and smiled and was glad that it had all happened. Then she danced away across the summer fields of heaven to Him Whose Name she had whispered on that day so long ago . . . her Jesus!

All will be well for those who love God. Now go to sleep.

9

SAINT GERARD MAJELLA

- The Skinny Kid Who Made It Big -

A young man rushed out of the bishop's house with a statue of the Infant in his arms. Quickly he reached the well, took the rope off the bucket, and made a knot around the statue. His lips moved in prayer as he lowered the statue into the well. He was still praying when he drew it up.

Happily, Gerard Majella saw a ring of keys on the Infant's finger. He untied the rope, and while the big crowd of people who had gathered cried out, "Miracle!" our hero quietly took his statue and the keys back to their owner. You bet your life he was happy, because he was the one who had accidentally dropped the keys into the well, and those keys belonged to his master, a rather cranky bishop.

Yes, it was a miracle, but you had better get used to miracles, if you want to read about this saint. After all, it is God's world, and if He wants to move His laws around a little bit when His best friends, the saints, get into trouble, well, it is His world, and nobody can do anything about that!

And another thing we have to face up to right now, young ladies and gentlemen, is that Gerard was a good boy. Yes, we can't get around it. He actually OBEYED! Of course, all this should not be too surprising, for what is a saint except a GOOD MAN, and just as in music or anything else, you have to start practicing when you are real young. So, Gerard practiced being good. When his mother called him, he actually came as soon as he heard her voice. Or does that sound like another miracle to you?

Of course, to obey—and all that—is not done just to be able to say we did it or to keep from being clobbered by our daddy. You have to be holy, not just because the catechism says so, but because of Someone. Otherwise, you don't have the real reason for being good, and you will find that your goodness will not last very long. You don't find martyrs dying for a catechism. Gerard caught on while he was very young that Our Lord was the real reason; and because Gerard loved Him, everything Our Lord said was the last word for Gerard. And because Gerard honored his parents, which is the 4th Commandment—your parents probably know that one, whatever they said was the last word for Gerard, too.

While we are talking about holiness in a child, there was one more thing that was very special to Gerard. He really loved to make visits to Our Lord in the Blessed Sacrament. Actually, he had a sort of reason that you do not have, which was that in those days, you could not make your first Holy Communion until you were about 12 years old, and then you could receive Our Lord only a few times a month. So, Gerard would run into church and tell God he loved him and wished he could receive Him right then, and that he would as soon as he could.

Like every young person, Gerard often thought of what he would be when he grew up. I guess we would naturally think that he wanted to be a priest and stay very close to Our Lord. Maybe so, but it is a bread-and-butter world, and the way things stood, Gerard had no brothers, so it was up to him to learn from his father how to be a tailor, so he could help his mother and sister someday. Studying for the priesthood would be a full-time job and would take lots of money. So, instead, Gerard put his time to tailoring, for thus he could support the home, in case anything happened to his father.

A very good man named Pannuto began to let Gerard help him in his tailor shop, and things did look rosy for a while. But, believe it or not, it was Gerard's prayers and visits to the Blessed

Sacrament that got him into trouble. Oh, Mr. Pannuto was very glad to have the pious young lad, but the shop foreman had different ideas and would pretty well wallop Gerard whenever he found him praying. Gerard had to sit down and figure out this new twist. Imagine begin beaten up, not because you were bad, but because you were trying to be good and holy! But Gerard figured that God was allowing this, so he would be all right. This was what "God's will be done" meant! This is how God got his saints! So, Gerard decided to go all out for it, and one day he was even smiling as the foreman was hitting him.

But let's get away from these one-sided boxing bouts and let Gerard's life open a bit for us. He did want to go and live in a house of religion as a monk, but his bad health would always be against him. He tried, when he was 16 years old and again when he was 18, to be a Capuchin religious. He was refused both times, because these religious houses would be sort of foolish to bring in someone to work if that person looked like he was ready to collapse. Gerard did look bad. He had lung trouble and actually would die from it before he was 30 years old.

So, Gerard went along in his life as a tailor, taking care of his mother and sister, giving anything extra to the poor and having Masses said for the souls in purgatory. But he was not really happy. Four words, "God died for me," seemed always in front of his eyes, and he was driven with a great desire to do anything and everything for this God who loved Gerard so much. Then in August, in the year 1748, something happened that would change his whole life and give him all he desired.

In that month, the Redemptorist Fathers came to Gerard's hometown of Muro. Our saint was especially interested in Brother Onofrio, the Redemptorist lay Brother who accompanied the Fathers and was doing all the side work that made the main work possible. Gerard followed him around endlessly, discovering that the Redemptorist Brother took the same vows as the priests, lived in the monastery with them, and did all kinds of work, such as sacristan, cook, tailor, doorman, gardener, and so on. Of course, it was the old story again—Gerard's poor health. So, Onofrio spent most of the time telling Gerard how tough the life was, full of hard times, self-denial, and heavy work. The more he talked, the more Gerard was convinced that, at last, he had reached his goal. He attended the mission that the Fathers gave, and when he viewed his life against the picture of eternity and heaven and hell, he wanted all the more to make sure of his eternity by becoming a Redemptorist Associate Brother, as they are now called.

Father Paul Cafaro, a great and holy priest, was the Superior of the mission, and he reacted strongly against taking in this weak-looking young man. Gerard's mother joined the battle and went to beg Father Cafaro not to accept him. The priest agreed with her and told her to lock Gerard in his room when the Redemptorists left Muro so that he could not follow them.

His mother did lock him in his room, and the plan worked fine, as far as the door was concerned. Gerard went out the window, tying sheets together for a rope to let himself down. He ran on and caught up with the Redemptorists 12 miles outside of Muro. He begged and begged and was refused and refused. He would not give up but tagged along after them, making himself as helpful as possible when they stopped to give a mission. He ran errands for them, did the dishes, and must have pretty well managed to be under everybody's feet. To make a long story short, Father Cafaro finally accepted him, in order to get rid of him. That is to say, he believed that Gerard himself would discover that his health could not stand-up to the difficult work and penances of the Redemptorists. In a famous letter, Father Cafaro wrote to Father Lorenzo at the town of Iliceto: "I am sending you another Brother who will be useless as far as any work is concerned, for he has a very delicate constitution."

And thus the religious life began for St. Gerard. Little did the priests and Brothers imagine that he would become a model for all the Brothers, that he would fulfill completely the founder's idea of the perfect Brother: "They are the sailors who work with the oars while the pilot and others are busy in the interior of the vessel."

The Brothers work with the conviction that no duty is too small, and that sin alone is degrading. Not *what* one does in God's service is the thing that counts, but *how* and *why*. Evidently, they must be very humble, or they will find they are in the wrong place. Just to set the record straight, Gerard was all this and more, and the priests and Brothers were soon very happy to have him. They all said that he "did the work of four." And that meant not just tailoring but taking his turn as carpenter, cook, sacristan, gardener, and doorman. And which one did he like best? You bet your life it was sacristan, for then he had every right and duty to spend his time around the altar and close to his beloved Lord.

In all monasteries there is a rule book telling the priests and Brothers and Sisters (in a convent) just how they are to go about their daily lives. It was once said that if all the Redemptorist rule books were lost, Gerard could write the whole thing for them, because he knew it by heart. For him, it was God's will to be done this day, this way. Maybe you youngsters think that obedience is just a big "do" or a big "don't." Really, there is something sweet and strong about knowing that you are doing what God actually wants you to do right now. Then comes a marvelous strength to go ahead and obey. St. Gerard was a great example of this. One time when he was sick in bed, his superior was about to leave and preach a mission. He needed Gerard to take care of the house, so he told him to get well. Gerard got right up, and the fever left him.

"How long should I stay well?" he asked the priest.

"Until I return," came the answer. And this is the way it was.

Sometimes things became a little weird. On one occasion, the superior, Fr. Fiocchi, was speaking to a bishop about St. Gerard's great obedience. The bishop said he would like to meet him and

asked the priest to send him over sometime.

"No need to wait," came the reply, and, in his mind, the superior commanded Gerard to come to the bishop's house at once. Sure enough, pretty soon there was a knock at the door, and who was standing there but Gerard. Yes, he was so anxious and ready to obey that God even whispered the commands to him ahead of time. About obedience, Gerard once said: "What the angels are doing in heaven, we do on earth." And don't you youngsters forget that, when it is your turn to set the table tonight.

However, don't be thinking that everyone walked all over Gerard. No, sir. He even once used his wonderful gift of miracles when a blacksmith tried to charge him triple price for putting shoes on his horse. Gerard refused to pay and told the horse to take off the shoes. Old Dobbin just reared up and shot off all four shoes and trotted away.

In God's eyes, this humble, sickly, little man was really a giant—for God. After all, size and health mean nothing to a Creator before Whom we are all tiny, helpless children. Yes, Gerard was a giant for God when it came to that great enemy of God—sin. He hated it. He slammed it wherever he found it. He fought it fiercely for souls. When no one else could bring around some great sinner, the cry would go up, "Get Gerard!" And he would come and produce. To him, sin was like an earthquake, a terrible disaster.

But he could love, too. He loved Our Lord very much. He deeply understood that the Tabernacle is only the "lodging house for Christ on earth; His real home is in man's heart." I do not mean that he no longer visited the Blessed Sacrament in the Tabernacle. Far from it. Before he became a Redemptorist, he used to borrow the key to the church in Muro, so he could pray when the place was closed. The day was not long enough, so he would borrow from the night. After he became a Redemptorist, the Tabernacle was in the chapel of his very house, and he no longer had to visit Our

Lord as a neighbor.

But St. Gerard knew that we really prove our love for God by loving people. He actually once made a promise always to give the best to others and to keep the worst for himself. And there is a big order for you youngsters. The simple answer is that he loved to see others happy. So, people loved to ask him for things.

So that is the story of St. Gerard. But only part of it. As many a mother knows, the story goes on and on, every day, and Gerard has become the patron of mothers. May he bless them all.

St. Gerard . . . his secret was simple. He loved everyone and everything that God loves.

Now go to sleep, you darlins.

10

Blesseds Luigi and Maria Beltrame Quattrocchi

- A Match Made in Heaven -

Maria and Luigi (not Mario and Luigi—get it right) were born 4 years apart. Luigi was born in Catania, Sicily, and Maria in Florence, Italy. Italy is pretty big, so the two did not meet for quite some time. Instead, they did what all children do: grow up.

Luigi grew up with his family until age 10, when his childless uncle and aunt wanted to adopt him. Since he loved his uncle and aunt, and they loved him, both he and his parents agreed. After that, he moved from Sicily to Rome.

Unfortunately, when Luigi arrived, Maria hadn't come to Rome yet. She was busy moving from town to town with her family because her father was in the military. He was a general with a short temper, while her mother was strong-willed, with little tolerance for attitude. This meant frequent quarreling, with Maria in the middle. To keep the peace, Maria once set the dinner table with olive leaves—a symbol of peace—tucked under her parents' napkins. "Papa," she blurted out, "I would never have married you like Mama did—with your bad temper!" Still, despite their flaws, Maria's parents deeply loved their only child. They raised her in the faith, sent her to school, taught her piano, and instilled in her a love for life. After 9 years of town-hopping, they settled in Rome.

It was there in Rome that Maria met Luigi. Their families became close friends in 1899, and the two bonded over their shared interests. In 1902, Luigi became a lawyer—the same year his adoptive father died. Shortly afterward, in 1903, his adoptive mother also died. Luigi was crushed by this loss. Left alone in the home, he spent more time with Maria's family. They took him under their wing, even inviting him to vacation with them in 1904. Unfortunately, Luigi got sick that Christmas—something "iggly-wiggly" with his intestines. It got so bad that Maria feared for his life. She sent him a picture of Mother Mary and wrote on the back about how much she cared for him. Luigi, who had little to no faith, got better and, with the help of Maria's love, grew to have faith in God. He carried that image with Maria's words for the rest of his life.

The two fell in love and were married on November 25, 1905. From then on, their days moved to a steady rhythm. Every morning, they went to Mass together. Only afterward would Luigi turn to Maria with a smile and say, "Good morning!"—as if to say, "The day can begin now that we have Jesus!" After breakfast, they parted for their daily duties, then met again at lunch. They parted once more, but at dusk they reunited for a half-hour walk, side by side, talking over the day. And every night before bed, Luigi gathered everyone to pray the Rosary, bead by bead, until the house settled into sleep (like you'll be doing soon).

Babies soon followed, one after the other. In 1906, Filippo was born. Then little Stefania arrived in 1908, followed by little Cesare a year later. Maria and Luigi made many small sacrifices for their children. For Maria, it meant fewer books, no theater for a while, and a lot more attention to the ordinary, while Luigi gave up smoking—much to his wife's satisfaction.

Then disaster struck. In 1913, when Maria was four months pregnant, she began to bleed. The doctor said that Maria had only a 5% chance of surviving and giving birth. The doctor—well respected, and a professor, too—urged Luigi and Maria to abort their baby. Shocked, both looked to Jesus on the Crucifix and gave their answer: a clear, loud "No."

Their home felt the strain. Stefania remembers her father weeping during that agonizing wait. For months after, Maria stayed in bed, not knowing if she would live or die. Instead of losing hope, the family turned their hearts to God and prayed. Then, on April 6, 1914, against all odds, baby Enrichetta was born. They called her their "miracle child"!

From then on, the house maintained what Cesare called "a supernatural, serene, and happy atmosphere"—with a rule that tough problems were "appealed to heaven." At night, Luigi continued to lead the Rosary; the Sacred Heart image held a place of honor on their mantel; and on the eve of First Fridays, they made a family holy hour. A steady stream of prayer kept the house warm.

Friends remember the house being filled with "noisy joy." The door was always open—that was the rule at Maria and Luigi's. Neighbors knew to drop by; the poor knew where to knock; and priests knew there was coffee and laughter waiting. Bitterness, resentment, and gossip were banned and when the children started whining with self-pity, Maria took them to hospitals to visit sick children and hand out candy. After seeing what others were suffering, their own tantrums soon disappeared.

Maria and Luigi raised four remarkable children, teaching them to live life, as they said, "from the roof up," which meant focusing on heaven. Their advice must have worked, because two of their kids became priests, one a cloistered nun, and the last, a lay-consecrated woman declared Venerable in the Church. Talk about a holy family!

When three of their kids left home, the two boys off to seminary—one in the morning; the other the same afternoon, and Stefania off to the cloister a few years later, it was hard on their parents. Maria wrote her children frequent letters, and Luigi visited each boy once a month, taking long weekend train rides. He also took up smoking again—much to his wife's dissatisfaction.

Over the 46 years of their marriage, through all the ups and downs, they never just sat back and let their faith collect dust. Some parents are content to drop off a can of beans for the poor and call it a day—but not these two. They were the kind of Catholics who rolled up their sleeves for God and started whole projects from scratch. In addition to Maria's work as a professor and Luigi's work in banks and state offices—including as deputy attorney general of Italy, they helped launch a group that carried the sick on pilgrimages so they, too, could pray at holy places. Luigi and his sons pulled together a scout troop for kids from the rougher parts of Rome, giving them purpose, play, and prayer. Maria? She filled notebooks and shelves with her books and articles for mothers and families, dove into Catholic Action projects, and even donned a Red Cross nurse's uniform in Ethiopia to care for the wounded. And on top of all that, they wrote each other mushy-gushy love letters—from before their engagement all through their married life.

When World War II broke out, Rome became dangerous. Luigi and Maria's apartment was just a short walk from the German headquarters. It was the wrong place to take risks, and yet no one in need was turned away. Jews, political refugees, and families in hiding and in danger all found shelter in their home. Their home stored false documents, and their sons' priestly garments disguised fugitives as they slipped past the Nazis on their way to safety in monasteries. In total, around 150 men and women were saved. Luigi and Maria sacrificed themselves, knowing that if they were caught, they would be shot.

After the war ended, Maria and Luigi moved to the countryside, where they enjoyed hiking in the mountains with their miracle child, Enrichetta, who cared for them tenderly in their old age.

On November 9, 1951, Luigi died of a heart attack at age 71, after spending what Maria later called "a last beautiful day" with his wife and daughter. For the next 14 years, Maria, with the support of Enrichetta, prayed, wrote, and served in any way she could. On August 26, 1965, after they prayed the Angelus together—the prayer recalling Mary's "yes" to God—Maria quietly passed away from a heart attack. She was 81 years old.

On Sunday, October 21, 2001, Pope John Paul II did something the Church had never done before: he beatified a husband and wife together. There in St. Peter's Square, under the wide sky of the Vatican, two sons and a miracle daughter watched as their parents were honored at the altar. Imagine that—being present for the day the Church declared your own mom and dad to be blessed! The novelty didn't stop there: the two sons, priests now in their 90s, were among those who concelebrated the Mass with the Pope.

Luigi and Maria's feast day is November 25. That's the same day as their wedding. But you didn't remember that.

Now, go to sleep.

Luigi and Maria Beltrame Quattrocchi as children, as a couple, and Maria with thier children.

Below is Maria in a Red Cross uniform. To her right are the Beltrame children from left to right: Cesare, Stephana, Enrichetta, Filippo, who became, in that order, a Trappist monk, a Benedictine nun, a consecrated lay woman, and a Benedictine priest. Below, far right are the two priest sons and Enrichetta with Pope John Paul II at their parents' beatification.

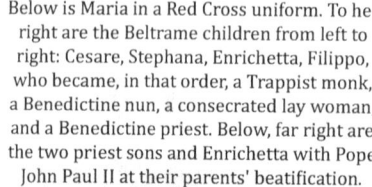

11

SAINT ANTHONY OF PADUA

- He Had His Own Tree House -

Many, many boys and girls are named Anthony and Tony, and Antonia and Antoinette. Let's talk about their saint: St. Anthony.

As a rule, everyone calls him St. Anthony of Padua, a town in Italy; but really, he was born in Lisbon, Portugal, in the year 1195, and I am not so sure that you are terrifically interested in that.

Actually, he is not just the saint of Padua but the saint of the whole world. Maybe you have learned that already. Did you ever lose something, and instead of screaming to your mother, you prayed to St. Anthony? Believe me, he is *The Great Finder*! Sometimes he seems to miss, because he is probably somewhere else looking for something for somebody else. (Just kidding, saints in heaven can help tons of people on earth, all at the same time). Or maybe you did not thank St. Anthony for the last time he got you out of trouble when you didn't know where "you had something last." (Just kidding, the saints, just like God, don't hold grudges.) St. Anthony is always on your side.

The Great Finder's last name was actually Bulhoes, but in those days, it was very important to be as royal as possible, and it seems that Anthony's family and their name was not any too royal. So, later on, those who wrote about St. Anthony changed his name a bit and gave him a few pints of blue blood for good measure. "Blue blood" are words used to show that there were kings or queens or nobles somewhere up in your family tree. But all that happened after Anthony was dead; let's talk instead about the live Anthony, who surely was not worried about royalty, except that of his real king, Our Lord.

What did St. Anthony look like? Lots of pictures and statues of St. Anthony make him skinny and dying from holiness or something, but if you ever go to Lisbon where he was born, you will find that many of the statues there show him as a fat, little altar boy. Today, the Lisbon children still look the same way—chubby, shoe-button eyes, sort of taking it easy, and always ready to break out into laughter.

Our saint had one big gift that you and I may not have, he was great at remembering things. Years later, in his sermons, he would bring in things he had learned as a young child. He was lucky because sometimes you and I have a hard time remembering something a week after it happened.

Anthony grew up and wanted to study to be a priest. He began at a place near his home, but it did not work out so well. It seems that his old buddies even came out to the seminary to talk him into leaving, or at least into joining in their wild times. Then Anthony did something that really showed what kind of a young man we have on our hands. He got up his courage and asked to be moved away from these old friends, even though it meant leaving his parents, his hometown, and all. Oh, we can read these lines real fast, but, if we stop a minute and think, we see a young man really trying to stay close to Our Lord at any price. We all have a few tough moments like that when we have to choose God's side, no matter what. Let us ask *The Great Finder* right now to help us find the way to God and stay with God.

Whenever you see a picture or statue of St. Anthony, he is dressed as a Franciscan priest, one who follows the path of St. Francis of Assisi. He did not begin that way. Instead, he was a follower of another saint—Augustine—and was quite happy in that life. Then one day, down the road came one of St. Francis' Brothers, as they are called. It was a very happy Anthony who listened to the story of these new Brothers, or friars. Like their founder, St. Francis of Assisi, they were actually taking Our Lord at his word:

"Do not have gold nor silver nor money in your purses nor two coats. Leave all, and follow me."

Through St. Francis, God had sent a new breath of fresh air into this old world. His followers grew and grew until there were 5,000 of them, just 10 years after they began. And now our Anthony wanted in, very much so. This desire became stronger, and it reached a boiling point when the caskets of five Franciscans, martyred for Our Lord in a place called Morocco, were brought to Anthony's convent. He begged for the Franciscan habit, which means the gray clothing they wore at that time. And he wanted to go to Morocco and be a martyr right away. Well, he got all the permissions in one day, and he would go to Morrocco, but not to be a martyr. We'll talk about that later.

The new life was not easy. These traveling Brothers had no money, no homes. They would work in the fields, fix falling bridges, take care of the sick, and eat whatever people gave them, sleeping wherever they could.

About Morocco: Anthony did go there, but the first thing he did was get sick, and those in charge knew he could never work in that weather. Back home he went, with a shipwreck thrown in for good measure. Quietly, Anthony decided to quit asking for what he wanted and let God put him wherever He wanted him. Our saint was a simple little man, the kind who might pass you by in the street, and you would say, "There goes a good man."

Saints don't have to be beautiful and handsome and all that. Their beauty is inside their hearts.

The Franciscans had a big meeting in Assisi, and Anthony quietly looked on. When it was all over, everyone left for his town and place. Anthony was left standing there. They had forgotten to appoint him to anything. Think of that the next time you are passed up, young man and young lady. Anthony just swallowed hard and waited till they picked him up and took him to his new home. The funny thing about all this was that Anthony had studied and read real hard and knew a whole lot, especially about the Bible. Nobody knew this, so he was given a real small job in the kitchen and that kind of humble work. Well, there was another big meeting, and, somehow, they had forgotten to have a speaker ready. The situation was so bad that they had to ask Anthony to preach. He did, and he wowed them. That did it. He was taken out of the kitchen and sent out on the road to become a great preacher.

Did St. Anthony do wonderful things like miracles during his life? We will tell you some of the things that are written down. There was one man who had become pretty bad, and Anthony told him to stop talking against our belief that Jesus is in the Host. The man said that he would starve a mule for three days and bring it near the church. Then, if Anthony would bring out the Blessed Sacrament, the man would put food before the donkey, and if the donkey refused to eat, then he would quit being against Our Lord. What happened? Three days later, the donkey was led to the church, and even though it hadn't eaten for three days, it did not even look at the food. Instead, it knelt down and adored Jesus in the Host. The man realized that the donkey was trying to tell him something, and he came back to Christ.

Guess which animals Noah left out when he put all the beasts in the Ark? The fish. I did not think of that either, until I read St. Anthony's beautiful sermon at the seashore. He told the fish that God loved them, so he let them swim right along with the deluge. Your mother or father will explain the deluge to you.

And it looks like Anthony managed to be in two places at one time. He was giving a sermon somewhere, and right in the middle of it, he remembered that he was supposed to be miles away in his convent, ringing the bell for prayer time. Anthony reached around and pulled his monk's hood, called a cowl, down over his face. (It sounds kind of silly.) At the same moment, he was seen ringing the bell back in the convent. Then our saint pushed back the cowl and went on with the sermon. You will have to figure out that one for yourself, but there were plenty of people who saw him in both places.

There was also the time that he was invited to dinner by some people who were enemies of the Church. Rather unhappy, Anthony brought up the point that the food was poisoned. The bad guys quoted the Bible: "If they drink any death-dealing thing it shall not harm them." They said they were really only trying to help Anthony honor God. Our saint gave them a smile, and then he caught them in their own trap. He said he would eat the food, and if it did not kill him, then they must all believe in the full Christian faith. They agreed, Anthony blessed the food, ate it, stood up fine and healthy, and bowed to the new full Christians—we hope.

I like the story in which one of the young Brothers was running away from the convent. Not having any money, he picked up some sermons that Anthony had just written and took them along, hoping he could sell them. Our saint came to his room and could not find the sermons anywhere. (He could hardly pray to himself as *The Great Finder*.) At that moment back came the young friar, all out of breath. He told Anthony that an enormous dark figure had stopped him and yelled, "Go back or you die." Anthony got his sermons, and the Brother found his way back to his vocation.

One last story. This was the time that Anthony was preaching to about 30,000 people in the open air. A terrible thunderstorm began. The people looked up helplessly. St. Anthony shouted for them to stay where they were, and they would not get wet. He went on to give his sermon, and when the people, all still dry, left for home, every square foot was covered with mud, water, and hailstones. They might have forgotten the sermon, but they would never forget the miracle.

You might think that Anthony spent most of his life in Padua, since he is called St. Anthony of Padua. Actually, he came to Padua just two years before his death, but the people there seem to have had a special love for him. There he would die when he was just 36 years old. Yes, kiddo, *just 36*!

During his time in Padua, there took place the big mix-up about the body of St. Francis of Assisi. In those days, towns would do battle with one another to see which one would be the burial place of a holy person. St. Francis' body was supposed to be brought to church from its first resting place. Lots of the royal people and the Franciscan superiors were going to be there. Then there was a wild rumor that the next town over planned to steal the body of St. Francis. Everybody started yelling and running. They picked up the coffin and rushed to the church and buried him in there three days before the big procession was to start. Anthony tried to stop them and took a terrible beating for his trying. Anyway, the people of Assisi got their little St. Francis.

And now for a terrific surprise that I have saved for last. St. Anthony had a *tree house*! Yes sir, he had a real favorite tree near the convent, and he loved to sit beneath it and write and pray. Then he got the idea that it would be much better to be up in the tree than under it, and sure enough, he drew up the plans and had some Brother carpenters build a first-class tree house way up in the limbs. There was another Brother who wrote down Anthony's sermons. Now he also wanted a tree house. But Anthony made him get his own tree, because he wanted to be alone. There must have

been a lot of hollering going on from tree to tree when our saint yelled his sermons over to him.

Today all the world calls St. Anthony the wonder-worker, but when he was alive, it was his preaching that made him famous. The reason for this was that he knew the Bible so well. One Pope, Sixtus the Fifth, said that if all the Scriptures in the world disappeared, you could still find the whole Bible in Anthony's sermons. He was an honest speaker and played no favorites. His language was beautiful, and, yet, he seems to have been so strict with the people that one writer wonders what it was about him that makes him so beloved. Maybe it was because he always liked to bring the Blessed Mother into his sermons. There is something we want and trust in a man who loves her.

One thing is sure. The great God honored the preaching of this man, for when his casket was taken up some years after he died to be given a new place of reverence, all of his body had turned to ashes, but *his tongue was completely unchanged*! It is still there today. And how do you like that?

One last moment. As you grow up, you will hear lots of people say that Friday the 13th is a very unlucky day. Our little St. Anthony doesn't think so. That's the day he went home to God forever.

Now go to sleep!

12

SAINT CLEMENT MARIA HOFBAUER

- The Baker Who Would Not Quit -

Many years ago, a little boy sat with a lot of other little boys while their pastor told them the glorious story of David and Goliath. Our little boy (whose real name was John, but would later be changed to Clement) was listening, mouth open, like you do when you hear about Wonder Woman or Superman. Goliath was a giant and David was just regular, so the odds were against him. Of course, we know the great victory that came to David when he held up his slingshot and put a big stone right in the middle of Goliath's forehead, finishing him off, once and for all. Johnny Hofbauer stood up and yelled, "Hooray for David!" And that broke up that catechism class.

This lad would always be a fighter (this does not mean fists), and he would always be found in the corner of the underdog. He simply would never be willing to stand by and do nothing for the hurt, the poor, the sick, the forgotten, and the down-and-out. Even while still young, there in his native land of Austria, he one day got into a barrel of trouble: he tried to help a gypsy lady whose husband was beating her because she had let herself get caught while stealing. Little Hofbauer ran up and sank his teeth into the man's hand. The fellow turned and beat the tar out of young John with a whip.

Very slowly Johnny would come to see and admit that, although we cannot very well stop the bad things in this world that are done by evil persons, we still might do something for the people who were hurt by the evil ones. And this was the beginning of Johnny's vocation to the priesthood.

He would never stop trying to help others until the day he died.

Of course, a vocation to the priesthood or Brotherhood or Sisterhood is not simply a matter of sitting back and wishing for it. You have to grab at every chance you get to move forward each time God gives you a little push. One of the best pushes for John, as for so many boys who become priests, was serving at Holy Mass. He loved to move in close to the altar on the big feast days and be lost amidst the great burning candles, the incense, the white Host.

Another push came from God, and Johnny jumped, when his pastor, seeing the boy's desire to be a priest, offered to teach him Latin—God's language, as Johnny called it. Everything really looked rosy, and then suddenly everything crashed. The old pastor died. Johnny remembered his last words: "Bring God's love to mankind, Hansl," he said, using the special loving way of saying "little John"—"Hansl."

But the Hofbauer family was poor, and in those days, a seminary was more like an ordinary high school or college, and you had to pay your way all the way—right away. There was nothing for him to do but take up a trade, and so off he went to learn to be a baker. The Bread of Life would have to wait a long time for Hansl. Meanwhile, he had to learn to make common bread. He lived with the common people and came to know their common sorrows and sufferings, so that someday he could help them all the more. Just the same, Johnny hung on to his old Latin books and tried to keep the words fresh by studying whenever he could find time outside of his baking.

John was not to spend his life in a bakery, so let us move along to one fine day when he decided he wanted to go to Rome. He and another young boy made their plans. Actually, there were not many plans to make. They had no money, so they would have to walk all the way there and back. But, before he reached Rome, John made a change in plans that would indeed change his whole life.

There was a hill outside the city of Tivoli, not too far from Rome, and on this hill, there was a beautiful little shrine of the Blessed Mother. The place was called Quintiliono, and it was tended by men who wore the robes of monks. The peace and beauty and chance for daily prayer and thought won over John. He decided to stay there. They took him in, gave him the robes, or habit, of a monk, and that was when his name was changed to Clement. Our new Clement was all ready to settle down. Meanwhile, however, the good Lord had no intention in the world of letting Hofbauer settle down on this quiet hilltop.

Yes, it was time for another push from God, and as Clement thought and prayed, day after day, it became very clear that he had no business sitting up here on a hill while the sorrowing world went by. He was made for the people, and the people were out there in their hungry lines, waiting for bread again, this time waiting for the Bread of Life—waiting for their Christ. Clement stood up and took off his monk's robes and slowly walked back down the hill. On and on he went until he came to an abbey. Here he knew there would be a great number of priests who could teach him, and he could pay for his education by working in the fields around the abbey.

By this time, Clement was no longer little Hansl. He was 30 years old—and there is a staggering number for you, young kiddo, to try to make peace with. He was much older than his classmates, and they sometimes were rough on him, and made fun of him. He had been through too much to let that worry him. He had a built-in grin like a porpoise, and sooner or later, people discovered that they liked him. His kindness and love for others began deep in his heart and came tumbling out all over the place.

Meanwhile, Clement's real troubles were about to begin. He is surely a wonderful example and model for a young man who finds his efforts to become a priest pretty rough sledding. For instance, suddenly out of a blue sky, there came a letter from the Emperor Franz Joseph telling the head priest that they could ordain no more men from that abbey. Heartbroken, Clement headed for the hills. He built a little hut and was about to give up all hope of ever becoming a priest.

And so the good Lord had to give him another push, this time from his own mother. She heard about his new disappointment and went out looking for him. She had prayed too many years for him to throw it all away. At last, she came upon his hut, and she really gave it to him, telling him to get going and to stop sitting there, wasting his life. "Get out and trust the Lord to guide you." (Hooray for mothers!)

The only trouble was, where could he go? He knew but one thing, baking, and so back to the old bakery he went. And then he ran into a brand-new kind of trouble. The baker's daughter began to think he would make a pretty good husband for her. The baker did, too, and sort of pushed things along a little. Clement saw which way the wind was blowing and finally had to break down and tell the baker that he had his heart set on being a priest.

"Oh," said the baker. "Oh, fine. But you are too poor to pay for your studies. You must be waiting for a miracle!"

"I am," answered Clement. And it came. It came from the deep faith and thoughtfulness of Resl, the baker's daughter, herself. When she realized that Clement really wanted to be a priest, she got up her courage and told his story to two wealthy ladies, the Von Maul sisters, who were regular customers at the bakery. Out of the blue sky, they decided—"Yes, they would pay his way at the University of Vienna." Clement had his miracle!

Off he went now to continue his studies. In Vienna he met an old buddy, Thad Huebl, who also wanted to study to be a priest and was also too poor to pay his way at the university. Enter again the good Von Maul sisters, and both young men found themselves happily back at the books.

But not for long. You see, the university was not a seminary, and some of the professors were teaching some weird stuff, especially about the Blessed Mother and the Immaculate Conception.

Clement and Thad took it as long as they could and then just got up and walked out of the classroom.

They knew where they were going. A man named Alphonsus Liguori had begun a missionary order in Naples, Italy, and he was now in Rome. Both Clement and Thad had read his writings, and they went looking for him. They did not stop until they stood there in Rome, knocking at the door of the Redemptorist Fathers, the group of priests (and their great helpers, the lay brothers) founded by St. Alphonsus. There in Rome, they completed their theological studies.

God had given them the last great push. He had taken the biggest rocks off the road for them, and now it was up to them to walk down that road. In a way, that is what a vocation is, God taking away the big rocks that might stop you, rocks such as real poor health that would keep you from going on, rocks like real poor grades in school that would make it too tough for you in higher studies, rocks that have to do with your living alone for Our Lord. And when He does take away these big rocks, and gives you, along with a sincere desire, good health, good studies, and the answer of your confessor that you should go ahead, then it is up to you to get going like Clement did. The big rocks are all gone, the little rocks you can step over, maybe trip over sometimes, but you keep going and you stop crying. Souls are out there waiting for you.

Finally, the great day of ordination came, and little Hansl was Father Clement Hofbauer, the Redemptorist missionary. One man above all, the great and holy Alphonsus, was deeply happy that day. He was already 90 years old; he had been growing afraid for the future of his congregation of priests, but now he cried out: "God will do great things through Fr. Hofbauer and Fr. Huebl."

Nor did the good Lord wait long to put the two of them to work. They were appointed to take the Redemptorist congregation (this word means the whole group – the Fathers and Brothers) across the Alps, the mountains, and give it a new foundation, a new house, in their own homeland of Austria.

The rest of our story, dear children, is going to make it pretty clear that God does ask a lot of his saints. We don't live on this earth very long, and He wants us to use up every minute of it for Him and His beloved humans, and He makes us sort of pay as we go. That is, you pay by your own suffering for the souls that you save. Clement surely did.

For one thing, Clement's mother died even before He got back home, though she died very happily, knowing that He was a priest, at last. When he did get to Vienna, it was the old story. The Catholic Church was having a hard time, and Clement was pretty well handcuffed. Finally, his superiors told him to try to help out in Poland. So, they went: Fr. Clement, Fr. Huebl, and a young novice, Peter Kunzelman. They walked through the snow and ice for hundreds of miles and arrived in Warsaw with three dollars between them and no idea of the Polish language.

The archbishop did give them the Church of St. Benno, but the church was about as badly off as the people. They could and they did scrub and clean up the church, but the people were much harder to scrub and clean up. Practically no one came to Mass on Sunday, and so Clement decided that if he could not get the grownups, he would go all out for the children. And he did. He started a little school for poor children, even taking in and caring for a dozen orphans. And how did he feed them? He went out and begged for them everywhere, anywhere. One day, he went into a tavern and asked for some money or food for the little ones. One man spat in his face. Clement fought his temper and conquered. Then he looked at the man and said: "That was for me. Now please give me something for my orphans."

It was a beginning, for that very same man took up a collection and sent the money to Fr. Hofbauer. Of course, the priests were still trying to get at the grownups, too. They went out and preached on the street corners. People would throw stones at them, they would be laughed at, but the next day, they would turn up again, their heads bandaged, still preaching away about God's love for us all. Pay as you go, and it began to pay off. In one year, the confessions at St. Benno went from 2,000 to 20,000. The church grew beautiful as the people began to put a little something in the collection box. Clement loved to decorate the church, loved beautiful church music, and the people began to crowd in.

Meantime, war was going on all over the place. If it wasn't the French, it was the Russians; but St. Benno stood strong. The church never closed. Confessions were heard all day long. About this time, some of Clement's enemies said that he was a spy. He thought it was a good idea. He would be a spy for God. He got out a map and decided where else he could start up the Redemptorists. How about France, Switzerland, Bavaria? Good! And surely enough, he began a foundation in each place.

Everything collapsed again. Dear little Napoleon was all over Europe; the head, the superior, of the Redemptorists was in a prison in Rome; all the new houses of the congregation, established by Clement, were closed down. St. Benno in Warsaw was the only Redemptorist place left freely functioning in the world! And then, finally, it happened. On the night of the feast of Corpus Christi, that terrible knock came at the door!

His enemies had won out. The orders were: "Give up being Redemptorists, and you can stay in Warsaw. Otherwise, you go to prison." The devil himself hated the Redemptorists. They were doing too much for our Lord and souls.

Later on that night, Clement gathered his brothers together, his Redemptorists. Suddenly, one of them, Podgorski, who as a soldier had carried in battle the last flag of Poland, ran to the statue of St. Paul and took a sword from his plaster hands.

"Swear on this sword," he cried to his companions, "that you shall be faithful to the Redemptorists and Fr. Hofbauer unto death."

Each one laid his hand on the sword and swore. In tears, Clement thanked them and then could only say, "And now, we are in the hands of God."

A few hours later five carriages came and took them to prison. Clement looked back on the ruins of 20 years' work. Pay as you go. And there was still more and more to pay before Alphonsus' and Clement's great dreams would come true, dreams of having the Redemptorists not just in Germany, but all over the world, even finding their way (in 1832) to the shores of our United States and there growing ever stronger as a great missionary congregation.

The time that Clement and his Redemptorist brothers spent in prison was very short, for the simple reason that they were sent out of Poland and back to their own countries. Once more, Clement found himself back in the old bakery. The bombs were still flying around, and one even landed in the dough that was supposed to be made into bread. The hospitals were filled with the sick and wounded, and our saint rolled up his sleeves and went to help, waiting on the sick, washing them, and taking care of them in every way he could. And once again, the crowds were lining up outside his confessional, and once again, he was helping the hopeless.

So, the days went by. Fr. Clement was not allowed to write to his superior in Rome. He was now 60 years old, and he was granted nothing but to say Mass at his Vienna convent and hear confessions. Then one day, he was permitted to preach publicly. It was like St. Benno all over again. The people flocked to hear him. They were tired and disgusted with all the fancy ideas about religion they'd been hearing.

"This man talks from his heart," they said. "He does not bother with proving anything. He talks as if he were there when it happened."

At 2 o'clock in the morning, he would rise and begin his prayer. "That is when the Lord and I bake our bread," he said, "and without that early hour of prayer, my hands would be empty all day."

But the baking was all done now, and as the Angelus rang out at noon on March 15 in the year of 1820, little Hansl ran back to God. And not empty-handed, either. For, even as he died, a messenger came from the emperor with a Letter of Decree bringing the Redemptorists into Austria. They put the letter into the lifeless hands of St. Clement Hofbauer, Redemptorist priest and missionary. But, really, they were a little late. He had already heard the news from St. Alphonsus in person. In heaven!

   Now, go to sleep, please!

13

SAINT BENEDICT LABRE

- The Homeless Man Who Tramped into Heaven -

Tonight, we tell of a saint who should be very popular with you young kiddos. His name is Benedict Joseph Labre, and it seems he very seldom got around to taking a bath. It was not that he hated to take a bath, the way you probably hate it. It was just the opposite; he would have liked lots of baths, but he had taken on the vocation of being God's beggar, and beggars don't often run into things like soap and towels and hot water.

    Our Benedict was the oldest of 14 children, and he grew up on his parents' farm at Amettes, near the French city of Boulogne. His story will not be of a great sinner turning back to God. Far from it, he went all out for God from the very beginning. His playmates found this out in a hurry when they tried any bad language or rotten talk around him. He simply loved God more than he did his playmates, so he told them off when they offended God out loud.

    Actually, he had run into those two words that you will meet a lot in your later life, namely, "human respect" or "peer pressure." They mean that you would rather hurt God than hurt human beings, so you give in to people, because you are scared of what they might say if they see you are trying to be good. It didn't bother Benedict much. He was not worried about what others thought. And yet, other children liked him. And do you know why? It wasn't because he was good at sports or something. In fact, he would rather pray than play. The reason was because he refused to be a phony. He simply believed that God was very, very holy, and so no one should be offending him.

Other children wanted to be his friend because he was such a good friend of God, and God is love. That was all there was to it, and any child will understand that right away.

Or maybe we can see it this way: Benedict thought that we are so little and God is everything, and we belong on our knees adoring Him and not standing up shaking our fist at Him. He also knew that if we lose something by staying God's good friend, He will make it up to us, since God is all goodness put together.

\As Benedict grew up, it seemed pretty certain to him, and everyone else, that he would study to be a priest. Lots of his relatives were in the priesthood, and, so, as was the custom in those days, Benedict went to live with his uncle, Fr. Labre, and began his studies. Benedict did study all right, but he learned more than Latin. His uncle was a man dear to God's heart, and he taught our young man about a thing called charity. That is another word you will be hearing all your life, so let's get it straight right now.

For some reason, we usually think that charity means giving away baskets of food to poor people on Thanksgiving or having collections for the foreign missions, and so forth. Well, it means that, but also a whole lot more. It really means loving God, but since God does not need anything, we show Him our love by giving ourselves and our treasure to those who need everything, His other children. Some people don't need a basket of food, they need our forgiveness; some people don't need our forgiveness, they need our kind words of encouragement; some people don't need encouragement, they need someone to tell them off, as Benedict told off the children who started bad talk.

On the other hand, Benedict and his uncle did not forget the kind of charity that gives to the poor. In fact, they gave away just about everything, even their table and chairs. That made quite a problem when they wanted to sit down, but they figured out a way around that little difficulty. The floor of their house was just ordinary earth, so they simply dug some holes in the ground, and then they could sit down and let their feet swing in the holes. This we do not suggest to any of you.

At this point in our story the road of our little saint's life took an altogether new turn. An epidemic struck the village, and Benedict's fine old uncle went home to God. For Benedict it meant the beginning of endless years of travel. The next few years would be spent trying to enter monastery after monastery.

In other words, Benedict had always felt that he should lead a stricter life, enter a great house of prayer and work, and live out his life quietly away from the world. That was not God's plan for him. Oh, he tried place after place. Sometimes his health was against him; other monasteries turned him down because he was too young. One group of Cistercian monks did bring him along as far as their novitiate (a place where vocations are looked into), and he was even given the name Brother Urban. It was not to be. His health failed once more, and he was sent home.

But he never got home. Instead, he turned south toward Italy. He wrote one letter to his parents when he stayed a while at the city of Piedmonte, and then he was not heard of again for 13 years. At the end of those 13 years, he would be dead, and people would be coming over the mountains to France to look upon and reverence the home of him whom they called "The Little Poor Man," "The Saint," or "Our Benedict."

What happened during all those years? Well, Benedict found his vocation, and it was a rare one, indeed. To get a quick idea of it, we might jump back a thousand years, or so, to a man in Rome named St. Alexius. Alexius seems to have been quite well off, was supposed to get married the next morning, and suddenly disappeared. He became a wandering hermit. Those two words really do not fit together, because we always think of a hermit as one who sort of anchors himself down to some isolated spot and certainly does not go wandering from place to place. Alexis, and now another saint, Benedict, would carry their solitary places in their hearts and have room only for God, no matter where they wandered.

I hope no one is getting the idea that Benedict was some sort of bum. Far from such a life, it took mountains of courage to do what he did. You see, Benedict had to face the truth that he did not fit in a monastery. On the other hand, he really wanted to live in this world as a poor man, like Our Lord. So, there was nothing left for him to do but live in poverty out on the road. It meant a life of begging for food, a lifetime of being looked down upon by everyone, of being mocked and laughed at, even, as we shall see, by the children.

Benedict took for his motto: "God wills it." His *Creator* gave him the wisdom not to try to do it all by himself. Instead, he asked many wise and holy priests for guidance throughout his life. As a rule, they were all deeply surprised at what he was doing, but, sooner or later, they came around to his way of thinking and agreed that our humble man had a sound calling from God to his life on the streets. In other words, Benedict was not bullheaded. He was willing and happy to get all the advice and help that God would send him through others.

So down the road he went. He wore an old gray coat full of holes, and his other clothing was still worse. There was more leather on the top of his shoes than on the bottom. There was no use in giving him anything decent to wear; he would simply find someone who needed it worse than he and pass it on. He wore a rosary around his neck, and the rest of his traveling gear was a little pouch that held a Bible and a book of church prayers.

Down the road he went, praying at each step, head bowed. Most people never saw the color of his eyes. His sleeping place was usually under a hedge along the side of the road or in a stable. He was sometimes invited to stay in a tavern inn, but the language was too rough for him, so he thanked them and kept going.

One thing we have to face up to: Benedict was not easy on the nose. (Yes, you could smell him coming and going.) He knew it, and it hurt him since he came from very neat, clean parents. But he took it as part of his sacrifice for God and souls. That is all we can say; he simply accepted the bugs and the dirt as part of the picture of his special way of walking through the world, as if it were a track with no other meaning than to get him back to God. How can you argue with that?

There is, however, one important thing to remember . . . he was always very careful not to deliberately hurt the feelings of others. He had made his place, and he would stay in it, alone. Just for an example, he would wait until everybody else had gone to Confession before he approached, so that no one would be offended by the tangy condition of his person. He was just the opposite of some well-meaning people who find a way of holiness that they like and then try to rope in everybody else. These half-saints can be whole thorns.

At times, things got pretty rough for our saint. He knew what it was like to be followed by mobs of children and laughed at. Stones were thrown at him. At least once he was seen to pick up and kiss the rock that hit him. He would not turn the boys in to the police; he simply thought that he suffered too little for Our Lord, as it was. Nor can we doubt that, in his younger days, grown people looked down on him because he did not get a job and build a decently comfortable life in this world. Benedict just took their looks, hung his head, and walked on. It would have been a lot easier for him to be poor for Christ's sake in a monastery with many brothers who were also poor for our Lord. Benedict's way was different, poor and alone, as was often Christ Himself.

True, sometimes it was the other way around. Some, wise in the ways of God, could see through the whole thing and realize how close this poor man was to Christ and would quietly tell others that they had a very holy man on their hands. Once again, Benedict would move on in a hurry. He was not in this business for kind words and backslapping. He was no phony. He was poor for Christ, not for congratulations.

When he found himself in Rome at nighttime, he loved to seek out a resting place beneath the arches of the Coliseum. This was the great arena where the circuses and the races were held. When Benedict rested there in the moonlight, he was not thinking of circuses but of the Christian men and women who had died out there on that in arena during the time of persecution. He envied them, even as he was dying for Our Lord in his own way.

Benedict had two special loves, serving Mass and encouraging the sick and poor. His day was happy if a priest let him serve his Mass despite his condition. For the poor sick he had a strange gift. He did not give them long talks all about putting up with the suffering and sorrows of life, but rather he left them full of pep to go along with whatever the loving God sent them. And you know that was the only kind of medicine that worked for them. Benedict used this gift to turn sunsets into sunrises. He had other special gifts from the Holy Spirit. He was also said to have cured some of the other homeless people he met and to have multiplied bread for them.

If we might try once more to make sense out of Benedict's life, then let us try once more to understand our Lord's words. He put all of our saint's life and struggles into one sentence: "The kingdom of heaven is like a merchant looking for fine pearls; when he finds one of great value, he goes and sells everything he owns and buys it."

Benedict had found his pearl of great price. He found God on earth in Jesus Christ. For this, he happily threw away everything. As we say, he bet everything on one roll of the dice. He did not think he had very much to throw away in the first place, any more than you or I. Our "all" is mighty little to give up for the great pearl of having God in our hearts now and always.

We will bring our little story to a close with a word about Benedict's great love for the Blessed Mother's home in Loreto, Italy. He had made 11 pilgrimages, or trips of penance, to this holy shrine, and, on the last journey there, he knew it was good-bye to Loreto and soon to the world. He made rounds to his few friends there, and, as he said good-by to them, they asked him, as they always did, about his next return. This time his answer was different: "I am going to my country."

The world was about to lose its very dear beggar.

Benedict went back to Rome, back to the end of his road. It happened during Holy Week, in April of the year 1783, just as he came out of the Church of Santa Maria dei Monti, he fell back against the steps, hardly conscious. A good man named Zacarelli picked him up and brought him to his home. Benedict did not realize that after 13 years, he was actually in a real bed at last. But Benedict had other things on his mind, in his heart, for, as the Angelus rang out, he came to the end of his road, and there, at last, he saw before him his beautiful country. And our country, too, please God.

Now go to sleep!

14

SAINT MARTIN DE PORRES

- The Barber Who Became a Saint -

Can you imagine a dog, and a cat, and a mouse eating out of the same bowl at the same time? Well, they did; and here is the story of the man who got them to do it.

These are the days and nights of St. Martin de Porres (pour-rays), and we shall find that he was a great barber, a great sweeper, and a great saint who loved people and animals. His love for all of God's creatures is the story of his life.

St. Martin lived some 400 years ago. His mother was a beautiful black woman, and his father belonged to the family of the king of Portugal. Martin was born in Lima, the capital city of the South American country of Peru. His mother was very devout and taught her children to be children of God. And while we are speaking of his childhood, we might run into here a little problem that may come your way. Martin had been taught to love the poor, but sometimes he overdid it. His mother would give him money to buy food for supper, and he would often give it all away. That was not so good because then his mother and sister had to go hungry. Kindness is not really kindness when we hurt someone else in the picture.

Martin's father wanted him to become a barber. In those days, however, a barber did more than cut hair. He did most of the doctoring in the neighborhood. He would fix up broken legs, give out medicine, and cut hair, all in one sitting. In fact, that's why—even to this day—the barber's pole seen outside his shop looks like a huge peppermint stick. (The white and red pole represents clean bandages wrapped around a bleeding wound.) Martin studied to be this kind of barber—not to become famous, but because he loved people and wanted to take pain out of their lives.

So, Martin went to school to learn his trade, but there was a different kind of schooling that the boy's heart was really wanting. Deep down, day by day, the call came louder and louder. Martin wanted to go to the school of the love of God. He wanted to enter a monastery, a place where he could give himself completely to God and His plans. Nothing and nobody could stop him. On the Cross our Lord cried, "I thirst." So did Martin. He thirsted for the souls for whom Jesus had died, and he wanted to fill up the thirst of our Lord with the love of people like you and me. Martin knocked on the door of the Dominican Monastery of the Holy Rosary in Lima. He was about 16 years old.

With his father's great name, de Porres, Martin could have gone up very high in the Church. Instead, he deliberately became a donado. That is a Spanish word, and in English it would simply mean a donation, a gift. Martin would not become a priest or even a Brother who helps the priests in their work, but instead, he would be a servant of priest and Brother. He would work in the fields, sweep the monastery, and just be a gift to God 24 hours a day. Martin would never turn back from his donado, his gift of himself. He was firm, not stubborn. (Mother, please explain the difference.) We all have a right to choose our way of life, and Martin stood by his choice. Someday he would be the greatest glory of the family de Porres.

Meanwhile, back at the monastery, he became a great sweeper. He did not like dirt, and he swept up everything that was not nailed down, so to say. No job was too grimy for him and his broom. And even to this day, the people of South America wear tiny brooms on his feast day.

But, in truth, the doctor side of our saint was called for more and more. Martin did not mind this at all. He knew that sickness could really be painful. When you hurt yourself—even a little finger—your body can hurt all over; and you don't feel much like praying, do you?

So Martin always hurried to help those who were hurting. Of course, human beings are kind of ornery sometimes, and they would yelp when our barber-doctor touched a sore spot. One time, when Martin was taking care of one of his Brothers, he must have pressed too hard where it hurt, and the Brother cried out: "Take it easy, you good-for-nothing!"

Martin said to himself, "This one really knows me and tells me off. I must take special care of him, so he will keep me in my place."

As you can see, we have a pretty humble donado on our hands. But that was nothing next to what happened later on. It seems that the monastery was running out of money and food and everything. The superior put together a few of the rare old treasures of the monastery and went out to sell them. Martin heard about it and ran down the street after the superior. He caught up with him, and all out of breath, he told him that he, Martin, could be sold as a slave, and then the treasures could be kept. The superior looked at him, and his eyes filled with tears. "Go home, my son," he said. "Brother Martin is not for sale."

What was happening in the soul of Martin all these days? This, for sure: his faith became very alive to him. Most people go into a church and barely notice the statues as they walk by. Not so for Martin; these were the people of heaven, crying out to him, "Come on! If we made it, you can. Courage!" (How about that?)

He asked the Blessed Mother to teach him how to pray. He surely learned from the best, and pretty soon he was able to pray even as he worked all day and half the night. Lima was a beautiful city, but it was loaded with sin, so Martin offered up his work and prayer to make it as beautiful inside as it was on the outside. He kept his own inside beautiful by going to Confession and receiving

Communion. For him, Confession bathed and clothed his soul, and Communion strengthened him to remain clean and pure. No wonder that people who knew him said that just looking at him made them want to do better.

What was his greatest gift to you and to all children? Obedience would be it. Obedience was not a lot of "don'ts" to him; instead, it was a big beautiful "do." And "do" meant to give his whole life in obedience to our Lord, just as our Lord spent his whole life in obedience to His Father. Obedience, by the way, does not mean that everybody is trying to push us around. No, it means that God has some things He wants done on earth, and we agree to get them done for Him while we are here, the way Martin did. Remember that, the next time your mother wants you to go to the store or do the dishes.

The more Martin gave himself to God, the more God gave Himself to Martin. There were times when God lit up his mind in wonderful ways. For instance, on more than one occasion, while Martin was sweeping the halls of the monastery, he came upon some students deep in a problem they had in class that day. Martin would politely listen, give them the right answer, and get back to his broom. The students would just look at him, amazed. They knew he had never studied such things.

Martin's whole life brought out another great truth, namely, that busy people always have time to help, while lazy people spend twice that time explaining why they can't help. Martin did not believe in those slippery answers, such as "Wait a minute" (meaning several hours from now) or "I'm busy now, come back tomorrow" (meaning never come back).

Now it is time to tell you about Martin and his animals, especially about his treaty of peace with the mice. This is really something, and it actually happened. In the monastery, Martin had charge of the clothing and sheets, and all that. Every night, however, a big gang of mice would feast on the cloth, and our Martin knew that this could not go on. One night, he waited up in the dark and finally caught one of the little fellows. Martin had quite a talk with him. He told the mouse that if he, the mouse, would keep his gang out of the clothes closets, then Martin would feed them every day at the other end of the garden.

It seems that the mouse went back and talked it over with the other bad guys; and then, suddenly, mice came from out the woodwork, the floor, every place, and all headed for the garden. The story had a happy ending; the mice kept their part of the bargain and Martin kept his.

There was nothing really so strange about this. If God loves His lilies, why shouldn't Martin love God's mice? They are all His creatures. And we can see now why it was not so hard for Martin to talk the dog and the cat and the mouse into eating together. In fact, there was one time when one of his Brothers heard Martin tell a cat to come back to the monastery the next morning for a checkup on his broken leg.

The Brother could not believe his ears, and was Johnny-on-the-spot the next morning, waiting to see what would happen. Sure enough, the cat was sitting there outside the door, and behind the cat was a turkey with a broken wing. Word really got around in the animal underground. Of course, they all knew that Martin would not hurt them, but you youngsters must not forget that our saint was very special. No child should ever pet a dog without asking his parents. (Not the dog's parents, silly!)

If we check out all the stories about Martin and his friends, it seems that the mice were his favorites. In fact, there are hardly any pictures of St. Martin in all of South America that do not have a mouse somewhere in them.

Meanwhile, many people came to visit Martin. Among them were the king's representative, the governor, the mayor, and all down the line. They came to him for advice, and at one time it was said that Martin was the power behind the throne. With the wisdom of a true child of God, he helped to run the great city of Lima.

He managed to keep his great gifts to himself as a rule, but there was one time when he almost let the cat out of the bag. (Not a real cat!) He was talking over a certain sickness with some doctors, and these words came out: "Yes, I saw this case treated in France." The doctors looked at Martin. They all knew he had never been out of South America. At least, they thought they knew. Actually, God had, in His own way, let Martin look in on the sickness and the cure in a French hospital.

With all this, it should come as no surprise that Martin once leaned over a dead Brother and whispered in his ear, "Brother Thomas!" And one hour later Brother Thomas was eating breakfast. Oh, yes, we have quite a patron saint for barbers and for everybody else.

This is the way that Martin lived. And when it came time for him to die, he felt, like so many saints, that life was such a short time in which to serve God and people and bring his love to them. Please God, that someday you, too, will carry Martin's burning torch of faith and love.

Now go to sleep.

15

SAINT CATHERINE LABOURÉ

- She Ate a Relic and Saw Mary -

On May 2, 1806, in a small village in Burgundy, France, called Fain-lès-Moutiers (pronounced . . . I give up), a little girl named Zoé Labouré was born. Her parents gave her that name, unaware, of course, that she would one day be known as St. Catherine Labouré of the Miraculous Medal. But first, Zoé had to grow up feeding chickens, milking cows, and doing all the usual French farm-kid things.

Zoé's family was big—really big. Eleven children. Sadly, when Zoé was only 9, her mother died. Losing a mother is like losing the sun—you still have light from the stars, but it's never quite the same. In her pain, Zoé turned to her Mother in heaven: the Blessed Virgin Mary. She climbed up on a chair in her family's home, reached for a statue of Mary, hugged it, and said, "Now, dear Blessed Mother, you will be my mother." Mother Mary would not forget little Zoé's heartfelt statement of pure faith.

At the age of 12, Zoé became the mistress of the household, a role that most women did not reach until their 50s—if ever. Under her father's oversight, she was given authority over the farmyard, the garden, the bakehouse, the orchard, the cowshed, the pigpen, the henhouse, and the dovecote—a tall structure with up to 800 birds and 1,121 pigeonholes for them to nest in. But that was only the outside of their large family property. Zoé also ran the inside of their sprawling home, making and serving meals for her family and snacks for the dozen farmhands, while looking after her two younger siblings.

At age 14, Zoé began the habit of fasting every Friday and Saturday, all year long, and frequently traveled on foot to pray alone in a small church in Fain. She had a secret dream—and it wasn't about becoming the best chicken-chaser in Burgundy. Zoé wanted to give her life to Jesus as a nun.

But there was a problem. Her dad. Pierre Labouré was not what you'd call supportive. He was strict, set in his ways, and could be downright stubborn. Dealing with him was an advanced course in patience. When Zoé announced she wanted to become a religious Sister, he didn't say, "Yes," or "Maybe," or "Let's pray about it." He said something in French—probably a lot like "Never"—and sent her off to Paris to work in her brother's café, hoping she'd get distracted with pastries or something and forget about becoming a nun.

But Zoé's heart didn't change. In fact, God gave her a dream to make her determination even stronger. One night, when she was 18, she dreamed of a gentle, noble-looking priest she had never met before. He motioned for her to come closer. "My daughter...," he said, "...one day you'll be happy to come to me. God has plans for you. Do not forget this!"

When she woke up, the dream stayed with her like a good melody you can't stop humming. Later, she would see a portrait of St. Vincent de Paul, the founder of the Daughters of Charity. "That's the man from my dream!" she exclaimed to herself. God was calling her to be one of St. Vincent's Daughters.

With extra doses of patience and perseverance, Zoé finally entered the convent of the Daughters of Charity at age 23. On April 21, 1830, she was given a black bodice tied at the waist, with a gathered skirt, and a black bonnet with wide white trim. From that moment on, she would be known as Sister Catherine Labouré. Her happiness was so great on that day that she felt "no longer on the earth."

Sister Catherine began her novitiate, which is a period of preparation, at the motherhouse on a street called Rue du Bac in Paris. The days started before the roosters could be bothered to crow, but she was used to that. Up she'd get, off she'd go, straight to the chapel for morning prayers, and then it was time to work. Then pray. Then work some more...

This was normal. What follows is not. Sister Catherine had a unique idea. She desired with all her heart to see the Blessed Virgin Mary, and she had a strong sense that St. Vincent de Paul would help her with this. On July 18, 1830, she was given a tiny relic, a scrap of cloth from his surplice, a white outer garment that he wore. She picked up the relic, tore it in two, took one piece—and she ate it. (Kids: do *not* try this. Relics are for veneration, not for snacking.)

Something worked, because that same night, when the convent was wrapped in a dark, peaceful stillness, and all were asleep, Sister Catherine was awoken by a child's voice calling to her: "Get up promptly and come to the chapel. The Blessed Virgin is there waiting for you."

Sister Catherine opened her eyes to see a little boy dressed in white, about 4 or 5 years old. She slipped out of bed, dressed quickly, and followed him down the corridor. Everywhere the child walked, the darkness seemed to pull back a little. She soon realized that the boy was her guardian angel.

When they reached the chapel, Sister Catherine saw that every single candle and candelabra was lit, their golden flames flickering like stars in a private sky. She knelt to pray. After a few suspenseful minutes, she heard the sound of rustling silk. And there she was—Mother Mary. She walked in and sat down in the director's chair beside the altar, her appearance more beautiful than words could handle.

Moving before she could think, Sister Catherine sprang up like a little girl and was at Mary's side in a single bound, resting her hands on Mary's knees. Finally, she could look into the eyes of the

Mother she had been loving for so long. Those moments, said Sister Catherine, were the sweetest of her entire life.

They spoke for two hours. Mary told her that God had a mission for her, that there would be challenges, but that His grace would never fail her. She spoke of France, of the trials to come, and of her desire to shelter her children under her care.

When the conversation ended and Catherine returned to her room, nothing looked different — but everything had changed.

Four months later, Sister Catherine was again seized with a conviction that she would see the Blessed Mother: "I thought that she would grant me this grace, but this desire was so strong that I was convinced that I would actually see her at her most beautiful." Then, during evening prayers on November 27, 1830, a familiar light filled the chapel again. She looked up, and there was Mother Mary in the sanctuary, hovering in the air in front of her! This time, she was standing on a globe, with rays of light streaming from the gems of rings on her fingers. She revealed to Sister Catherine:

"These rays symbolize the graces I shed upon those who ask for them. The gems from which rays do not fall are the graces for which souls forget to ask." Then an oval frame formed around her, bordered with the golden lettered words: "O Mary, conceived without sin, pray for us who have recourse to thee." The image revolved to show a reverse side. A cross above large M appeared, and below it, the two Hearts of Jesus and Mary—the first crowned with thorns and the second pierced with a sword. Twelve stars encircled the entire oval tableau. With a tone of command, Our Lady stated:

Have a medal struck after this model. All who wear it will receive great graces; they should wear it around the neck. The graces will be abundant for those who wear it with confidence.

Excited and scared, Sister Catherine told her confessor, Father Jean Marie Aladel, about the apparition and Our Lady's request for a special medal. "Pure illusion!" he scolded. "If you want to honor Our Lady, 'imitate her virtues' and beware of your imagination!"

"You will have plenty of suffering," the Blessed Mother had told her.

Only days later, in mid-December, Mary appeared to Sister Catherine again above the Tabernacle, looking just as she had a few days before with her "hair parted down the middle," her robe "the color of dawn," and a "blue veil." Again, Sister Catherine heard in the depths of her soul: "These rays of light are the symbol of the graces that the Blessed Virgin obtains for those who ask them of her."

The apparition vanished with a farewell. "You will not see me anymore," said the Blessed Mother, "but you will hear my voice during your prayers."

Then, just like that, the light faded. Sister Catherine was left kneeling in the dim chapel, her heart both full and aching. She would never again see her Mother in her lifetime, plus a heavy burden had been laid on her shoulders and carved into her soul. The Blessed Mother had been crystal clear: she wanted a medal made, and she wanted it spread everywhere. Sister Catherine couldn't exactly do that on her own. She had to go back to Father Aladel and try to convince him! No easy task.

Because she had been so silenced on the matter, Sister Catherine didn't bother mentioning Mary's third apparition. But she did make Father Aladel promise never to reveal to anyone her name or identity as the visionary who saw Mary. That was no problem for Father Aladel, because he didn't believe her anyway. How on earth was Sister Catherine going to get this Medal out to the whole world?

The novitiate ended for Sister Catherine on January 30, 1831. She made her vows and received her habit in the order of the Daughters of Charity, also called the Sisters of Charity. Have you ever seen pictures of those big white hats that they used to wear, called cornettes? They looked like wide paper airplanes or flying fortune cookies. Nowadays, the Daughters of Charity don't wear them anymore, probably because they couldn't fit inside anyone's car. Anyway, that's the cool hat that she got to wear.

With her secret for the world tucked away in her heart, Sister Catherine was assigned to Enghien Hospice, a retirement home for the poor, closer to where Father Aladel could keep an eye on her. And there she lived and worked for the rest of her life.

Sister Catherine didn't give up. Again, she tried to convince Father Aladel of the Blessed Mother's request. But when she walked into Father Aladel's confessional with her heart thumping and her palms sweating, he shut her down.

Frustrated, she told Mary, "He does not want to listen to me!"

The Blessed Mother looked upset and responded to her in an inner locution: "He is my servant," she said, "and he should be frightened of displeasing me." Sister Catherine wanted to run the other way rather than talk to Father Aladel one more time, but she knew that doing whatever heaven asked for was supremely important. She also knew that by avoiding what Mary was asking for, she would suffer even more, and the world would suffer, too. That's how it works, my little friends, when it comes to doing what God commands in our lives.

So, Sister Catherine obeyed Mary's wishes and told Father Aladel, "The Virgin is angry," and shared what she said about him: "He is my servant, and he should be frightened of displeasing me." Well, that must have scared the bejeebers out of him because, at last, something changed. He took the medal's design to the Archbishop, the Archbishop approved of it, and the first medals were made in 1832. A heavenly door had finally flung open, and Mary's prayers and influence swept quickly across the world. Miracles of healing, conversion, and protection began happening wherever the medal traveled. Because of this, it would eventually receive the name, the Miraculous Medal.

(If you would like a Miraculous Medal, you can probably get one, too. Mom? Dad? Be sure to get it blessed by a priest. That's what makes it effective. If you want Miraculous Medals that are already blessed—to wear around your neck, like Mary asked, or to give away—you can go to www.QueenofPeaceMedia.com.)

Here's the craziest part. For 46 years, nobody knew that Sister Catherine was the nun behind the medal—not the elderly she cared for, not the curious visitors who came to the hospice, not the nuns she lived with, not even her Mother Superior. When the Sisters would ask her, "Who do you think the secret visionary could be?" She pretended to be just as curious as they were. She kept the secret locked tighter than the convent door after curfew. She cooked and cleaned at the hospice, tended the cows, chickens, and pigeons that provided their food, and cared for the poor elderly with generous love—while the Miraculous Medal swept across the world, changing lives.

Let's be honest, Sister Catherine's ability to keep a secret is impressive. When it comes to most of us, if the Queen of Heaven had chosen *us* for a world-changing mission, and if we had to carry the burden of our confessor thinking, at least temporarily, that we were nuts, we'd at least "accidentally" tell our best friend. . . or maybe our cousin. . . or, you know, the mailman. But Sister Catherine? She waited until her deathbed to whisper the truth to her Mother Superior—and even then, she would have taken it to her grave, if not for a nudge from heaven.

The Mother Superior looked at the ailing visionary and asked her, "Aren't you afraid of dying?"

Sister Catherine's blue eyes of 70 years took on a thoughtful look of wonder, and she answered, "Why be afraid of going to meet Our Lord, His Mother, and St. Vincent?"

In 1876, the year that Sister Catherine died, her identity could finally be revealed. The hard-working, humble, and pious nun, who never sought to draw a minute of attention to herself, had been entrusted with one of the greatest of heaven's projects in all of human history. And now the world knows who she is—a saint, St. Catherine Labouré.

Now, go to sleep.

(To read the riveting full story of St. Catherine Labouré and fascinating stories of Miraculous Medal miracles from around the world, right up to the present day, see *The Miraculous Medal: Pendant of Power* at the end of this book.)

The statue of the Blessed Mother that Zoé embraced

Sister of Charity giving supplies to a destitute family

Dining room in the farmhouse

Pierre Labouré & Madelein Louise Gontard

Novices of the Daughters of Charity

Zoé's secret: every day, she stole a few minutes to pray in the little church in Fain

The actual chair on which the Blessed Mother sat

St. Vincent de Paul (1581-1660)

140 Rue du Bac

Nun showing love to an orphan

The only actual picture of St. Catherine Labouré, taken shortly before her death into new life

The Enghien Hospice

The Miraculous Medal, front and back

Father Jean Marie Aladel, Sister Catherine's confessor

Archbishop of Paris, Hyacinthe-Louis de Quélen

Novices on the left, professed Sisters on the right in the Chapel on Rue du Bac, 1800s

St. Catherine Labouré's incorrupt body

16

VENERABLE FRANCIS XAVIER NGUYỄN VĂN THUẬN

- Captivity Could Not Contain Him -

Francis Xavier Nguyễn Văn Thuận was born in 1928 and grew up in Huế, Vietnam. His family lived on the banks of the Perfume River, where on nights of full moons and festivals, paper lanterns with candles drift gently downstream, creating a glowing path of red and golden lights in the dark. Just like those lanterns, Thuận would carry the light of faith along the twisting currents of his life, especially into the darkness.

 Thuận's name is pronounced "Twan" and means "conforming to (God's) will." Imagine trying to live up to that name in kindergarten! His mother was named Elizabeth Ngô Đình thi Hiep, and his father, Thaddeus Nguyen van Âm. In Vietnam, names come backwards—first names are last, last names are first. So, we'll call Thuận's mom by her first name, Hiep, which is pronounced "he' up," and we'll call his father, Âm, which is pronounced "um."

 Hiep loved God. She taught wisely and she radiated holiness. She had memorized the entire French missionary catechism before age six, and even as a child, recited the Rosary so often, the beads probably prayed back. From his mother, Thuận learned very young to recite three Hail Marys and the *Memorare*, morning and evening, and to love God, Mary, and the saints with his whole heart. He also learned that he was cherished.

 From his father, Thuận learned patience—not because Thaddeus Nguyen van Âm had that virtue, but because he found fault with everything his kids said and did. When Thuận's brothers and siblings added up to 7, they nicknamed him "Thaddeus the Difficult." But Âm was a deeply faithful man, whose attention disappeared into deep prayer when at Mass with his family, and he made sure that everyone prayed together each evening in a chapel in their home. After evening prayers, Thuận's grandmother would pray another Rosary. When Thuận asked her why, she said, "I pray this Rosary for priests." She did not know how to read or write, but grandmothers and mothers like her shape vocations in hearts. One day her prayers would be answered.

From a young age, Thuận was inspired by the stories of his ancestors who were brave martyrs, willing to suffer for their faith. When Thuận was a young child, one of his favorite uncles, Ngô Đình Diệm, who would end up being the President of South Vietnam—twice, spoke to him about his bloodlines from both parents: "We are all men and women of faith. We are all descendants of martyrs, from whom we inherited courage and spirituality."

For Thuận, thinking about his ancestors filled him with courage. One of his favorite stories was about his great-great-grandfather, Danh, and his son, Vong, who became a legend in his own time. That was back in 1860, when an Emperor attempted to wipe out Catholicism and devised a plan called *phan sáp* which means "divide and integrate." This new policy split Catholic families apart from one another and then made them slaves in the homes of non-believers, in order to either starve them or force them to abandon their Faith. Not very nice, was it?

Vong's mother and younger siblings were sent away as household slaves; his father, Danh, was forced to work as an unpaid laborer; and Vong was sent to work in a rice field some six miles away from his father. Vong was only 14 years old. Somehow, Vong heard that his father, Danh, was being starved by his cruel landlord, So he went up to his own landlord and asked permission to bring food to Danh every morning. Vong did not stop to consider that he hardly received enough food to eat himself.

Every morning, when it was still dark, Vong woke up, cooked his small ration of food, and carried half of it to his father. This meant he had to run the *12-mile* round trip to be back in the rice field on time to begin work alongside the other laborers *at sunrise*. And he did this for *several years!* It's hard to believe, but it's true. Sometimes, when things are tough, God's grace combined with our love and selflessness gives us the power to do things that might seem impossible. Remember, St. Peter actually walked on water when he believed and trusted in Jesus. So, Danh was eternally grateful to his eldest son, who saved his life and made his hell endurable, and he was really proud that none of his children gave up their faith.

Eventually, the Emperor realized that his *phan sap* policy was more like a *sad phlop*, and he dropped it altogether. Nothing seemed to break the courage of the Vietnamese Catholics, who knew that by holding onto their religion, they were holding onto salvation. Nothing in the whole wide world is more important than that!

So Thuận was Vong's great-grandson. At age 13, Thuận decided that he, too, was ready to do great things. He mustered up some courage and sat down next to his parents as they were sipping tea in the living room. Taking a deep breath, he told them he wanted to be a priest. Hiep looked at her son and then looked away to hide her tears, since this meant that he would have to live miles away from home during each school year at a boys' high school seminary. Âm looked at him and then told him the food there was terrible, the discipline was hard, and because he was so spoiled by his mother, he wouldn't last long. Well, his father was right about one thing: the food.

Thuận ended up enjoying seminary much more than was expected, and he aced his studies. A language genius, he became fluent in Classical Chinese, Latin, and French. (French was a key language for theological studies in Vietnam, since French imperialists had colonized Vietnam by force, and French missionaries had introduced Catholicism.) Later, Thuận would tackle Italian, Spanish, and English. His talent for languages didn't stop there; he could mimic anyone, which means he could copy anyone's voice and the way they moved. This made his fellow seminarians crack up! Thankfully, they still let him graduate.

On June 11, 1953, in Hanoi, Francis Xavier Nguyễn Văn Thuận was ordained to the Catholic priesthood. He took the name "Francis Xavier" because, in our Catholic tradition, priests often take a saint's name as part of their ordination. His first assignment? A professor and spiritual director at the major seminary in Huế, where he was known for being joyful, charismatic, deeply spiritual, and tireless in his service. Thuận's vocation continued to grow, and grow, and grow. He was moved in the Church from priest to bishop, to archbishop, to cardinal, like one of the bright lanterns carried along the Perfume River. But it wasn't in high places that Thuận's light would blaze most brightly—it would happen in hidden places of crushing darkness.

The darkness came when the Communists started to take over Vietnam. You see, Communists believe in taking away people's freedom and forcing them to believe only what the government tells them. People living in Communist countries are not free to practice their faith, and Communists don't believe in God. They are atheists and believe that religion is very bad and threatening—especially Catholicism. They see the Church as their enemy, like a big four-eyed monster taking away their power, because the Church is an institution that they cannot control. Nor can they control that Catholics believe in a figure named Jesus, Who has all the power in the world. So, Communist governments try to "fix" what they see as a "problem." They stamp out whoever they see as their enemies, and they do it in big, violent, and bossy ways.

When Thuận became a bishop, the Communists were already trying to take over Vietnam by force. "I was very active...," he said. "There was something that pushed me forward every day: to run against the clock, as it were, because I had to do everything possible to strengthen and build up the

Church in my diocese of Nha Trang before the hard times came under Communist rule!"

The Communists saw Bishop Francis Xavier Nguyễn Văn Thuận and his family as a problem getting worse. His parents and two sisters fled to Australia to escape the war at their doorstep, while Thuận received permission to rush to ordain all of the seminarians who were prepared. Bishop Thuận felt no fear on that day of ordination, as he spoke the prayers of Holy Orders, offering new priests to Vietnam's future. He felt thrilled. In his mind, he heard the voices of his grandfather and uncles saying, "We have to do what is right, and we are willing to pay the price." Do you ever have thoughts in your head, encouraging you to do the right thing? And then you feel good when you do it? Well, it was kind of like that for him.

While South Vietnam lay in ruins, and exactly one week before the fall of Saigon to Communist forces, Pope Paul VI elevated Thuận to Coadjutor Archbishop of Saigon. Just three months after he was named Archbishop and set to lead the Catholic Church in South Vietnam, his life took a dramatic turn. On August 15, 1975, the communist revolutionaries invited Archbishop Thuận to the Presidential Palace in Saigon. He was taken to a small room where several government officials were waiting. An interrogator started accusing him, saying, "You are a fomenter of troubles and a lackey for the imperialists!" Thuận asked them why he was getting all these labels.

Angrily, the interrogator shot back, "In this city and elsewhere, reactionary Catholics are saying that the Catholic Church needs a leader like you. Why are they saying this? Why does the Catholic Church need a strong leader? To fight against whom? Against what? Against patriots? Against the revolutionaries? That is why I called you a fomenter of troubles!"

Thuận told them that he didn't do anything wrong.

Then another official screamed in his face, "Did you hear me? I told you to admit that your appointment as Archbishop of Saigon is a plot designed by the Vatican and the imperialists!" Thuận shook his head in disagreement, telling them none of it was true. But the Communists did not believe him. They wanted him punished for a crime he did not commit.

So Archbishop Thuận would spend the next 13 years in prison—9 of them in solitary confinement. He would suffer long years in a damp cell, with extreme heat, no windows, no fresh air, little food, and mushrooms growing on his hard mattress. Sometimes the guards would turn off the light for days, and sometimes they'd leave it on. At one point, he was sent to a concentration camp, which believe it or not, gave him more freedom. But when they decided they didn't like his actions, they moved him back into solitary confinement. Thuận never knew how long he would be in prison, or if he would ever be set free. Later, he would write:

> Above all, I suffered the long tribulation of nine years in solitary confinement: seeing only two guards every day, enduring mental torture, absolute emptiness, with no work to do, having to walk back and forth in my cramped cell from morning to night so that I would not become crippled by arthritis. I was on the brink of insanity.
>
> Many times, I was tempted, tormented by the fact that I was 48 years old, in the prime of my life; I had worked as a bishop for eight years, I had acquired a great deal of pastoral experience, and there I was: isolated, inactive, and separated from my people by 1,700 kilometers!
>
> One night I heard a voice encouraging me from the depths of my heart: "Why do you torment yourself so? You must learn to distinguish between God and the works of God. Everything you have done and desire to continue doing: the formation of seminarians, men and women religious, laity, and youth, pastoral visits, constructing schools, atriums for students, missions for the evangelization of non-Christians . . .

> all of these are excellent works, they are God's works, but they are not God! If God wants you to leave all of these works, place them in God's hand immediately and have confidence in Him. God will accomplish things infinitely better than you..."
>
> I had always tried to do God's will, but this light brought me a new strength that completely changed my way of thinking and helped me to overcome moments that were almost physically impossible to overcome."

Thuận had finally seen the truth that God had been showing him. He repeated to himself, *"Choose God and not God's works: God wants me here and nowhere else."*

Thuận accepted his cross, not because he loved suffering, but because he loved Jesus. Taking a scrap of paper that was smuggled to him, he wrote:

> Beloved Jesus...
>
> I am happy, here in this cell,
> where white mushrooms are growing on my sleeping mat,
> because You are with me,
> because You want me to live here with You.

After that, Thuận's soul became a place of great light. He started to find joy in his extreme weakness and isolation, simply by loving God and letting God love him. Referring to the name he took at his ordination, "Francis Xavier," he wrote: "When my strength failed me, and I could not even pray, I repeated, 'Jesus, here I am. It's Francis.' Joy and consolation would come to me, and I experienced Jesus responding, 'Francis, here I am. It's Jesus.'"

So, youngsters, why don't you try this same prayer with Jesus right now? You don't have to do something great, or even do anything at all, for Jesus to love you and want to be with you. So, are you ready? Go ahead and say, *"Jesus, here I am. It's ____,"* and say your name. Then imagine Jesus saying back to you, *"[Your name], here I am. It's Jesus."* Try this a couple of times. Realize that Jesus is right there with you now! Mom, Dad, reader—maybe you can say the Jesus part?

Thuận thought back to a miracle he had received from Jesus about four years after he had been ordained a priest. His bishop had sent him to Rome in 1957 to get a doctorate in canon law—which has nothing to do with canons or the law, but don't worry about that right now. During his time there, Thuận became very ill. He was diagnosed with advanced tuberculosis and scheduled for surgery to have half of his lung removed—a procedure that could leave him an invalid—if he even survived it.

On the day of Thuận's scheduled surgery, the doctors took one last X-ray. They were flummoxed. The scan showed no sign of any disease. The tuberculosis was completely gone. Someone had once told him that God never wastes a miracle.

Thuận realized that, just like Jesus kept him alive then, He was keeping him alive now—all for a reason. Thuận was not destroyed because he had the actual Bread of Life in his cell with him. He was never alone. When he was first arrested, he had to leave immediately with empty hands. The next day, he was allowed to request in writing the things he needed most: clothes, toothpaste... He wrote to ask family: "Please, could you send me a bit of medicine for my bad stomach?" Many such notes would follow over the years. The faithful always understood what Thuận meant and would send a little bottle of wine, which they labeled "stomach medicine," as well as some tiny bits of unconsecrated hosts sealed in a bottle or flashlight to protect them from the humidity. With these treasures, the archbishop could celebrate Mass with a speck of bread, three drops of wine, and a drop of water, using his palm as a chalice. So, the Real Presence, Jesus Christ Himself, King of Kings, Lord of Lords, was always with him, physically, right there in the Eucharist!

Thuận also thought of how he was re-living through the Eucharist, the story of his great great-grandfather, Danh. Danh was persecuted for his Catholic Faith: he was sent to live with his enemy, given too little food, and confined for years, not knowing if his exile would ever end. Now, over a century later, Thuận was living a similar exile. He, too, was ill-treated, malnourished, and confined by his enemies with an unknown conclusion, all because of his Faith. But this time, it wasn't a 14-year-old son sneaking in to give him food and love, to carry him through a living hell. It was the Son of God.

Inspired by the miracle of Jesus' Presence with him and in him, Thuận continued to write spiritual reflections on scraps of paper, which were smuggled out by the faithful and ended up becoming several books, translated into many languages.

By the way, since Thuận lived not too long ago, you can actually see his face, experience his personality, and hear him speak about his time in Communist captivity. Check out an EWTN YouTube video by EWTN. Search for "The Late François-Xavier Cardinal Nguyên Van Thuận with Raymond Arroyo." No, not now! You can watch it later. (P.S., Mom. . . Dad. . . whoever is reading this. . . There's also a documentary DVD of his story called *Road of Hope: The Spiritual Journey of Cardinal Nguyen Van Thuan*, if DVD's even still exist by the time you're reading this.)

Ok, back to Thuận's life. This is where his story gets really good, and not so depressing. I picked out just a few things to tell you from his time in prison. . .

At first, Thuận was watched by a group of 5 police guards, 2 of whom always accompanied him in his solitary confinement. The wardens then changed the 5 guards every 2 weeks so that they wouldn't get "contaminated" by Thuận and *catch the Spirit*. Then the warden realized *all* of the guards were getting contaminated after just 2 weeks with Thuận, so he went back to guarding him with the same 5 guys. These 5 men would be Thuận's only human contact for seven years.

At first, the prison guards were under orders to never chat with their prisoner, and they answered his questions with a sharp "yes" or "no." This made Thuận sad because they were Thuận's only potential friends in the whole world. "I have nothing to give them," he worried. "Nothing, I'm too poor." But one night, an idea came to him. "Francis," he thought, addressing himself by his religious name. "You are still very rich. You have the love of Christ in your heart. Love them as Jesus has loved you."

So, Thuận began to smile at the guards and tell them stories about his travels. Because of his kindness, they grew curious, and little by little, the 5 guards became his friends. Soon enough, Thuận was teaching them foreign languages. And guess what? A section of that prison became something like *"Thuận's In-Home Language Academy."* Before long, the police chief started sending in more guards for "lessons." Too bad that learning a language couldn't help with "sentence" structures. Mom, Dad, did you get it?

One day, the chief asked the Archbishop Thuận what he thought of the newspaper, *The Catholic*. One question led to another, and Thuận ended up creating for him a *"dictionary"* of religious terms, from A to Z. What started as a detailed list quickly turned into a practical catechism, which knocked out many of the Communists' wrong ideas about the Catholic Faith.

Soon, the guards were wandering the halls of the prison, belting out Catholic hymns like *Veni Creator* and *Salve Regina* in perfect Latin.

Guards often got confused around Thuận because, as he said in the EWTN interview I told you about: "My first principle was to live in the present moment and fill it with love." This didn't make sense to any of them...

Left Photo: Thuận's family home in Huế

Family photo from left up to right: Thuận's mother, paternal grandmother, father, himself (kneeling). The rest, besides the man standing, are Thuận's siblings

Thuận, a seminarian at Phú Xuân Major Seminary, holds his yougest sister, Thu Hồng

Ordained a priest in 1953

On his motorbike at the Phú Xuân Major Seminary in Huế

Thuận was relocated for a time to a concentration camp, the Re-education Camp of Vinh Quang (Vinh Phú), where he was required to do hard labor outdoors, sleep in a bed with 25 men on either side of him, squished together like a pack of toothpicks, and attend Friday brainwashing sessions about the glories of Communism. There, in the mountains of Vinh Phú, one guard was willing to look the other way as Thuận carved a cross out of wood that he was supposed to be chopping. "You're hard to say no to!" said the guard, terrified for Thuận and for himself, because religious symbols were strictly forbidden. Thuân hid the cross in a piece of soap and kept it safe in his chest pocket always.

None of the guards could understand how it was possible for someone to forgive, to love one's enemies, to be reconciled with them.

"Do you really love us?" they would ask the archbishop.

"Yes, I sincerely love you."

Shocked, they persisted: "Even when we have treated you so badly? When you have suffered in prison for so many years without ever having a trial?"

"Yes, I still love you."

"That's impossible! Perhaps it's not true!"

"Think about the years we have been here together," Thuận insisted. "You have seen for yourselves that it's true. I really love you!"

"When you are freed, you won't try to take revenge on us or our families?"

"No, I will continue loving you, even if you want to kill me."

"But why?" they asked.

"Because Jesus has taught me to love you; if I do not, I am no longer worthy of being called a Christian."

Due to international pressure in his favor, Thuận was taken on May 13, 1978, to the small town of Giang Xa and placed under house arrest—or rather, dilapidated rectory arrest. Foreign pressure also allowed him visitors under the watchful eye of his guard, and all visitors from outside Vietnam had to be accompanied by the Ministry of Interior's representatives and interpreters.

Thuận did not mind the presence of official government interpreters. He spoke with his usual sense of humor and slipped in a few clues. For instance, when asked by a representative of Catholic Relief Services whether he was being treated well, Thuận replied, "The government always takes good care of me. A while ago, when I was very sick, a physician came to see me three weeks later." In another interview, he shared, "The government always shows their concern for me. As a matter of fact, I am always watched attentively by a hundred pairs of eyes."

The villagers in Giang Xa were told a made-up story about the evil archbishop who mercilessly shot down a group of Communist revolutionaries. So, at first, they hid from the "bloodthirsty" archbishop. But then Thuận, just being himself, caused a transformation—again.

To explain what happened, I have to give you what is called a back story—that is, tell you what was going on before Thuận got there. You see, in North Vietnam, the Communists had worked for years recruiting 4 or 5 Catholic families in each parish and converting the heads of these families to Communism by offering money, power, and privileges. These "Catholics" became the eyes and ears of the government, forming a spy network that caused many innocent Catholics to be arrested, convicted, and imprisoned. The worst of the spies in the village was a couple living just next to the town Church, who earned the sarcastic nickname, "the saints." But even they warmed to Thuận's goodness, sending him bowls of soup or boiled sweet potatoes. "Send their gift back," said Thuận's Communist guard-turned-secret protector. "They are evil. Perhaps they have put poison in the food."

Thuận laughed him off, saying, "Why don't we give them a second chance? Who knows what they will become if we are kind to them?"

One day, "the saints" asked Thuận to hear their confessions. He was astonished by their sincerity and made sure they were released from their excommunication from the Church. In time, the couple became very devout Catholics and joined the growing number of people keeping watch as the archbishop celebrated Mass for hundreds who now visited him. Word of his love and mercy spread underground, and repentant Catholic spies traveled from all over Vietnam to see the archbishop in order to confess their sins and be reconciled to God and the Catholic Church.

Eventually, the Communist authorities discovered that there was a complete collapse of their government's network of informants spying on the Catholic population. And it all pointed to one humble man held captive in the small village of Giang Xa. Back to solitary confinement he went.

One of Thuận's prayers while he was in captivity was to Mary. At times, he would say to her, "Mother, if you see that I can still be useful to your Church, then let me leave prison on one of your feast days!"

On November 21, 1988, it finally happened: Archbishop Thuận was released from his arrest. "Today is the Feast of Mary's Presentation in the Temple," he realized. "It is Mary who is setting me free. Thank you, Mary!"

Filled with immense joy, relief, gratitude, and a spirit of adventure, but still not allowed to venture far from Hanoi or return to church leadership in Vietnam, Thuận thought he might take a trip. A daring thought came to mind. He would try to visit his parents in Australia, who didn't know if he was alive or dead. He wanted and needed to make his visit a surprise, since his plans could be stopped by the Communists at any turn.

But Thuận made it all the way there! No one stopped or interrogated him on the way. Thirteen years had passed, but it felt like an eternity. Âm and Hiep were informed by phone that a "certain

Monsignor" wished to see them at 3:00 p.m. sharp. Âm responded without hesitation, "Please tell the Monsignor that we will be happy to see him." For years, Âm and Hiep had been welcoming cardinals, archbishops, and monsignors and had appealed to them to help Thuận.

They put on their best traditional Vietnamese outfits and were ready to receive the "Monsignor." The doorbell rang. Âm opened the door immediately. He stood motionless in absolute shock to see his long-lost son, Thuận, on his doorstep. True to character, Âm simply said, "Please come in, Monsignor!" Thuận stepped inside and was unable to move when he saw his mother. Hiep looked at him as though her eyes were fooling her, as if she was lost in a dream. Yet she couldn't stop smiling and saying over and over, "You are here. You are alive!"

After Thuận returned to Vietnam, he eventually realized he could not safely stay in his home country anymore. He sent a message to the Vatican about his situation. "Get out" was their response. In the early 1990s, Thuận began living in exile in Rome, and from there, preached around the world. On November 24, 1994, Pope John Paul II nominated him to help lead the Pontifical Council for Justice and Peace, of which he later became the president.

On January 19, 2001, Thuận was genuinely surprised when Pope John Paul II called to personally congratulate him on his elevation to the College of Cardinals. When the Pope announced the news from his window overlooking Saint Peter's Square, Thuận's telephone rang off the hook with calls of congratulations. When one friend exclaimed, "You must be so happy to have been chosen by the Pope for this honor!" Thuận instantly replied, "But I was already happy!"

The following year, on September 16, at age 74, Thuận passed away into a happiness that would not be taken away from him, ever again. His life had been a floating lantern—lit by the fire of his ancestors, carried by courage, and glowing in love, long after it disappeared into the night.

Now, float into sleep, dear ones.

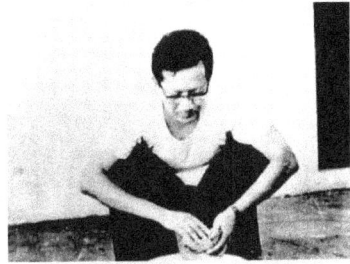
Under house arrest in Giang Xa

Walking to the door of his parents' home in Australia

Thuận astonished his mother and father, who did not know if they would see him again

Made Cardinal and embraced by Pope John Paul II

Cardinal Francis Xavier Nguyễn Văn Thuận

In his last days of preaching

Archbishop Francis Xavier Nguyễn Văn Thuận

Released from prison and ordered to live at the Archbishop's Residence in Hanoi

17

SAINT JOHN BOSCO

- Love Him, Love His Dog -

They say that a horse is man's best friend. But we think that a dog is a best friend when it comes to boys and girls. So, tonight, we are going to tell you the story of a man who had a mystery dog. We will talk about Don Bosco, the children he cared for, and, of course, his dog. So, let's begin.

First of all, about his name. John is his real name. The Italians call their priests Don instead of Father, so in our little story you will understand if sometimes we call him John, and sometimes we call him Don.

It seems that the best way to find out about anybody is to discover what his parents were like. They do that before you enter a seminary to be a priest. They figure that they can get a good idea of you that way.

In the case of little John Bosco, his father died when he was just two years old, so we will have to take a look at his mother. She is sure worth a good look. She was a wonderful person. Her Johnny was born about 165 years ago and was brought up among the beautiful mountains called the Alps. Johnny was born on an Alp.

Everybody called Mrs. Bosco "Mama Margaret," so we will too. She thought that one of the most important lessons for Johnny to learn was to say thank you to God, because it was a wonderful thing that God would let cows give milk and trees give apples. The earth is a kind of wonderful fairyland, and God just touches the earth with His wand, and the good things to eat and drink and wear pop up all over the place. Of course, the farmers help. It makes you think, for instance, what if God had forgotten strawberries or potatoes or hamburgers or pickles? But He didn't, so all the fairy tales help us to see how much God loves all of us.

Mama Margaret was a wonderful woman, and she was very close to God. She would spend a great part of her life being a mother to thousands of children who had lost their parents and had come to her son, John Bosco, for help. She was not very well educated, but she had the great gifts of love and common sense, and that is enough for anyone.

For some reason, as young John grew up, he often thought about hungry boys and girls who had nothing to eat or drink, even though while in the middle of all these beautiful gifts from heaven. They had nothing to thank God for, they thought, because they were always hungry. That was bad, little Johnny figured, and he began to hope that he could make helping orphans his whole life's special calling. Of course, God was doing the calling.

Maybe this is beginning to sound as if Johnny sat around all day just doing a lot of deep thinking. Not at all. He had once been taken to a fair, and there he sort of fell in love with what he saw: a man was walking a tightrope and others were doing juggling acts. He watched them all day long. When Johnny came home, he went into business for himself. He tied a rope real tight between two trees and began to practice. Day after day, he kept on trying until he was a really good tightrope walker. Then he started juggling, and after a while, he could put on a whole show by himself. And he did. The only price of admission for the children who came to watch him was that they must say 10 Hail Mary's with him before and after the greatest show on earth. No pray—no stay, was his motto.

Did Johnny act like a knucklehead in his childhood? Oh, yes, he had to learn like we all did. One day he and his brother, Joseph, came in from play, and they were very thirsty. Somehow Mama Margaret gave Joseph the first glass of milk. John grew very angry and would not drink any milk at all if he could not be first. His mother quietly put the milk away and went about her work, not saying a word to our young hero. Finally, Johnny boy could not stand it any longer, and he said to his mother, "Please give me a drink, too."

"Oh," she said, "I thought you were not thirsty."

"Oh yes, Mama." he said. "Forgive me, please."

Sometimes we all like to get bullheaded like John did that day, but our mother has to see right over our heads and not give in to us. Otherwise, we would go through life whining and being sulky until everybody gave in to us. If you are that way, and if you keep being that way, people will not like you, and they will not want you around at their parties and things.

Young John Bosco was growing up, and he began to think of the life of the priesthood. There was a fine old priest, Fr. Colosso, a pastor at a nearby town. This good man took a special interest in our young tightrope walker. One day, John Bosco told him that he wanted to be a priest, especially to help young children. And that is how, with the priest to guide him, John began his studies. God had given him a good brain, so he got through all those years of study without sweating too much.

Soon after the glorious day of his ordination, he was given an appointment that would also include visiting prisons. This is what would really ring the bell for John. He was shocked at seeing the jailbirds, mostly young orphans who had hardly been taught the difference between right and wrong, hardly knew why they had been sent to jail. These youngsters had little ahead of them but to be hanged someday when their crimes became great. Don Bosco rolled up his sleeves and began collecting orphans wherever he could get them. He wanted to do everything he could so that they would never land in jail and into a life of crime.

The way it turned out was that his biggest problem would not be talking boys into coming to him but finding a place where they all could come to him. Don Bosco and his boys were, well . . . they were booted from place to place. Nobody trusted these young lads dressed in their rags, and as a result, when Don Bosco did finally get a Sunday church for his growing crowd of young boys, they were soon told that the people living near the church did not want them around because "they might be a bad influence on their own children," and so forth and so on.

Came the day when he and his young crowd had to go out beyond the town. Their numbers grew—with the sky as their only roof. Don Bosco would talk to them. He would explain the catechism to them. He would help them go to Confession and then say Mass for them. For these poor children it was a grand time. They would all meet on Sunday, and Don Bosco would have a new place for them to walk to, and when they got there, they would play and pray and listen to our saint.

That Don Bosco and his children were unwelcome can be seen from this story. There were these two elderly men who tried to put our saint away in an asylum. They waited for Don Bosco one night with their carriage, and when he came out of the house, they asked him to get into the carriage. Don Bosco somehow smelled that something was wrong here, so he quickly turned around and shoved the two men into the carriage and yelled to the driver to hurry up and take them out to the institution and not to listen to them, because they were out of their minds. And, actually, the two tricky gentlemen were driven all the way out of town, and when they finally arrived and were let out of the carriage, they realized that Don Bosco was very, very sharp and not so very crazy at all.

So we see that Don Bosco had many ups and downs, and now it is time for one of the ups. His hope had always been to find a place where his boys could stay and be fed and learn their faith. A man he knew decided to let him use a shed, and when the neighbors complained about it, the king himself, Charles Albert, stepped in and commanded that Don Bosco and his boys be left alone.

This good news came almost too late. Our saint had become sick. Maybe he was just heartsick because of all the bad breaks that he had had. Then a priest friend of his came to see him and said, "You have to want your life for your little people. You must live for them."

Don Bosco looked at him and said, "You are right. I want to get better right now for my little people." And that is the way it was. The next day he was up and back to his life's work. Wanting is important, isn't it?

I hope you do not get the idea that this was all a grand picnic. Far from it. Some days, his boys never even got a glass of milk. Do you know where the orphanage really was? Don Bosco himself was the orphanage. Yes, he was sort of a traveling orphanage, because, in those days, they did not have foster homes to take care of children whose parents had left them or who had died. So, Don Bosco, the traveling orphanage, would pick them up on his way. Our saint loved these children, and when people called his little ones ragamuffins, as they did, then he would call himself "Chief Ragamuffin."

So that is the picture. The only church he had for many years was an old shed, and his only help was his mother, who had left all behind in her hometown of Becchi to come to keep house for her son. The kids almost drove her crazy, but she had a lot of motherly love. Once she said to her son, "I would not blame them too much; they didn't put all that life into their blood."

Gradually the school began to do better. The people of Turin, the big town in that neighborhood, began to see that Don Bosco was saving boys who might have become the crooks and the bad guys in their city. The money actually started to roll in.

Please do not get the idea that Don Bosco had his children sitting around all day. Far from

it. He taught them everything he knew, such as bookkeeping, shoemaking, carpentering, and, of course, above all, their religion. Did they gradually get rich and take it easy? I will tell you. If a boy had a spoon to eat with, he carried it with him all day, because he would never find another one.

Don Bosco would teach them their religion, but he never forced anything on them, including Confession. By kindness, and because the love of Our Lord was in his own eyes, he drew the boys to the Master. For example, one of the boys wanted to make a good Confession, and he wrote down all his sins, and then he lost the book with the sins in it. Well, he cried long and loud and was finally led to Don Bosco. He told the priest, "I lost my sins."

Everybody around him laughed, but Don Bosco said, "You are lucky. You should be happy. Don't ever find them, and you will go straight to heaven when you die." Actually, Don Bosco had found the book, and now he told the boy that he had it in his pocket and had only been fooling about losing them anywhere except in the mercy of God. The young eyes dried up quickly, and the lad began to laugh.

"Good," he said, "when I go to Confession tonight, I will just accuse myself of all the sins you have in your pocket."

And now we come to the part about Don Bosco's mystery dog. It was a very big mystery dog. We have noticed that our saint was often in trouble with certain people trying to trick him—some even tried to kill him. God gave him some help. Nobody knows where the dog came from. And nobody knows where he went. All of a sudden, he would show up to protect Don Bosco. It looks like God did it because Don Bosco had such very important work to do for children, and He did not want robbers and people like that to get in the way of our saint's work.

A good friend of Don Bosco, Mr. Buzzeti, tells us about the dog. He, himself, had often protected our saint; in fact, one time he put his hand in front of a pistol aimed at St. John, and the bullet knocked off his thumb. So, we can see that he personally was pretty happy to notice this dog taking over such a dangerous bodyguard job. The dog was gray in color, so Don Bosco called him *Il Grigio* which means in Italian "the gray one." The dog was kept pretty busy because Don Bosco's building was way out in the country, and there were not many streets nor many lights; he often had to get from one place to another and back to his own room late at night. Anyway, this dog was no little puppy. One night, two bad men were waiting for St. Bosco on a dark road, and then they grabbed him and gagged him and put a blanket over him. They were doing pretty well until Big Gray showed up, and then they did not know what hit them. The great dog hit them all right, growling like a grizzly bear, snapping and biting until the robbers begged Don Bosco to call him off. Don Bosco did, and the gray one backed up, still standing guard.

Whenever Don Bosco came home late, the dog would be near. He would come up to be petted and then walk along with our saint.

We said it was a dog of mystery. Well, one day Don Bosco came home from Turin, and it was quite late. Then he remembered he had forgotten some important business in Turin. He started to go out, and Mama Margaret begged him not to. He insisted. But when he opened the door, Big Gray was stretched across the doorway growling. He would not let Don Bosco leave that night. Mama said, "Look, the dog has more sense than you have." (Does that sound like your mom?) Well, it turned out that Mama and the dog were right because a neighbor soon knocked on the door to warn Don Bosco that he had seen some very mean people waiting for him out in the dark.

One night the dog came to say good-bye. (Of course, nobody knew that then.) It was suppertime, and, as usual, the animal would not eat or drink; he just wanted to lay his head on Don Bosco's lap and be petted. Then he went away, and believe it or not, he did not come back for 30 years.

One stormy night, he did finally come back to lead Don Bosco and another priest out of a swamp they had wandered into. Don Bosco had said out loud, "If only my Grigio were here," and suddenly he was there, waiting to be petted and to lead the two priests to safety. The other priest said to him later, "Why did you call that dog Grigio?"

Don Bosco answered, "Because it was my Grigio. It was his size, his color, he knew me and came up to be petted as he always did."

Let us talk a moment about Don Bosco's training of these young boys. He was not in this business to turn out children who were soft little puddings. He talked to them about the love of one's neighbor, carried out at any price, especially on one very serious occasion when an epidemic of something like the flu swept over the countryside. By insisting on cleanliness and lots of prayer, Don Bosco saved his children, although the hospitals were filled with the sick and dying throughout the district. Don Bosco gathered his youngsters and said to them, "Now we are going to pay back these people who have given us a new chance in life. We are going to the hospital and take care of them. And, if any of us should die, we will accept death for the love of God and for our neighbor."

We are very happy to say that, out of the 40 strongest boys that he had chosen to work in the hospitals, not one of them grew sick, and the people of the neighborhood were deeply thankful to our saint, at last.

One more word about Don Bosco's boys. At the time of his own death, not one of the thousands he had raised had ever been in trouble with the law.

If dear Don Bosco would tell me how to end this, I think he would say, "Write about the confessional." Because there he was happy, bringing souls back to our Lord.

Don Bosco even knew when he was hearing confessions for the last time. A group of people had come a long way to ask his help in the confessional, but the assistant priest told Don Bosco that he was too weak to hear them, and they should be sent away. Don Bosco thought for a moment and then said, "Let them in. It is the last time." And so it was. And that one sentence sort of sums up his life: "Let them in! Let my children in."

Now go to sleep.

18

SAINT CARLO ACUTIS

- The First Millennial Saint -

Well, children, you've already heard some pretty wild saint stories. There's St. Joan of Arc leading an army into battle, St. Kateri escaping from her own dad (who just happened to be a Mohawk chief), and St. Martin de Porres making peace with mice. With adventures like that, you might wonder, "Hold on—these people don't sound anything like me. They're so different! Can I even be a saint if my life is so… ordinary?"

The answer is: Of course you can! Saints come in every size, style, and century—including yours. God made you to be a saint in *your* own way. And tonight, let me tell you about one who lived not so long ago, so his life might look a lot like yours. His name was Carlo Acutis.

Carlo was born in 1991. (Yes, that's right—not the 1500s or the Middle Ages.) He grew up in a well-to-do area of Milan, Italy, in a family that was pretty wealthy. His mom, Antonia, came from a family of publishers, and his dad, Andrea, worked as an executive in his family's insurance company. True, most of us aren't born into money, but Carlo didn't have wild and crazy experiences like some other saints. Nobody chased him on horseback, he never started a fire with just a prayer, and he wasn't tossed into a Communist prison. But just you wait—you'll see how he managed to be extraordinary in the middle of a basically ordinary life.

Antonia and Andrea weren't sure what to do with their son, who seemed to notice God's love before his own shadow. Sometimes they felt like they were raising an alien. They weren't exactly the church-going type. In fact, before Carlo was born, they hardly ever went to Mass. They kept their schedules full but with no room for God. But then along came Carlo—and suddenly the parents were the students, and their toddler was the teacher.

From the start, Carlo seemed to know that Jesus and Mary were as real as the toys in his hands. This was a grace, a free gift, straight from God. But since his parents were too wrapped up in the world, God sent a Polish nanny named Beata to help Carlo's faith grow during his first 5 years. Beata read to him from his favorite illustrated Bible—a gift from his grandparents—and from books about the saints, like this one. She even taught him the Rosary and took him to Mass, where he'd get sad that he couldn't take Communion. Whenever she looked into Carlo's big eyes, she felt like she was seeing a cherub missing his wings.

And Carlo—he was full of surprises. He soaked it all up like a sponge. Beata tried to keep up with his "grown-up questions." While other kids were wondering, "Where's candy?" Carlo was asking, "Why did Jesus have to die?"

One time, Beata scolded him for letting some kids pick on him and not fighting back. Did Carlo yell, cry, or throw dirt in their faces? Nope. He answered her that Jesus would not have been happy if he had reacted with violence.

But Carlo didn't just keep his faith to himself. He dragged his parents along, too. Carlo spoke to his parents with respect and spontaneity, obeying them willingly—but he also obeyed the invisible nudges of God's Spirit. At first, he was going into churches with Beata and saying hello to Jesus. Then around age 4, he started tugging his mom into churches, as well, wanting her to go before the Tabernacle with him to greet Jesus. And when they took walks, he liked to pick flowers from the field and give them to the Virgin Mary. At home, he made Antonia pray the Rosary with him and tell him more and more about St. Francis of Assisi, St. Clare, and St. Anthony of Padua—his favorites.

Sometimes when he was alone, she caught him blowing kisses to the crucifix on the wall or the Infant of Prague in his room.

Antonia looked at her boy, so in love with Jesus, Mary, the angels, and the saints, and thought, "What planet did you come from?"

Carlo's Grandma Luana was looking after him one day, a few months after her husband had died of a heart attack. Suddenly, Carlo grabbed his coat and announced he wanted to go to church. Why? Because—he said with perfect confidence—his grandfather had come to him, dressed in blue, and told him he was saved but needed prayers because he was in purgatory. (Now that got Grandma Luana's attention!)

People were also surprised by Carlo's generosity. He'd give away toys if other kids didn't have any. He waited patiently for meals without tantrums. And when dessert came, he let everyone else take theirs first. Then, and only then, he'd have his. (Now that's heroic.) At age 5, little Carlo walked over to his piggy bank and dumped out all his coins. He gathered them up and handed them to a family friend, a Capuchin priest named Fr. Giulio Savoldi, who helped the poor. Carlo wanted all of his money to go to children who didn't have anything. Fr. Savoldi said that he had never seen a child so sensitive to poverty and the suffering of others.

Carlo helped anyone in need—young, old, gypsy, Muslim, atheist. . . In time, his friends got used to it: one moment Carlo was hanging out, the next moment—poof!—he'd spotted someone in need and dashed off, handing away his allowance.

Around age 6, he was walking his mom's yippy dog, Chiara, one day through Milan's beautiful Parco Solari, alongside Grandma Luana. There, he met up with a boy he had become one of his besties. Carlo noticed the red and swollen eyes of his friend's Filipino nanny. "What is wrong?" he asked her. She told him that in the Philippines her family's house had been destroyed by a typhoon, her mother had been hurt badly, and she couldn't pay for her care. Carlo immediately went to work. He took all the money out of his piggy bank. Antonia offered to help too, as long as he agreed to get one less present for his birthday. Happy, he brought the Filipino girl all the money he had collected. The girl embraced him and started to cry, saying that Carlo was the only one who had helped.

Was he absolutely perfect? Well. . . Carlo was also a showman with spontaneous energy. His teachers occasionally sent home notes about "lively chatter," "amusing comments," and "waving hands"—code for "he's talking too much." When he started doing an examination of conscience every night before bed, taking a close look at his thoughts and actions of the day, he dialed it down a bit. At home, he used his overflowing creativity to turn his housekeeper, Rajesh Mohur, into an amazing and somehow world famous "spy detective" who had to search for Carlo's hidden pets—four dogs, two cats, a turtle and some goldfish.

One day, when a nobleman who belonged to a chivalric order came to visit the Acutis family for lunch in their Milan apartment, Carlo got the giggles—inside. The man was dressed in the garments of a noble knight and had old-fashioned ways of speaking and moving. His chest was covered by so many medals that the material of his jacket was invisible. When the man left, Carlo disappeared. Twenty minutes later, he came back covered in paper medals that he had drawn himself and taped all over his chest, to make his parents laugh.

As you can see, Carlo was easygoing, good-natured, giving, compassionate, funny, smart, entertaining, and full of energy. But he wanted more—he wanted the *infinite*. His mom and dad could barely keep up. When he was 6, they hunted down books and documentaries on saints and apparitions, and Antonia started theology classes, cracked open a Bible and the Catechism, and even found herself a priest for spiritual direction. That priest, Fr. Ilio Carrai, was rumored to be another Padre Pio. When she sat down across from him, he looked at her and said he had been *waiting for her for years!* He also told her that Carlo had been *chosen by God for something special.* (Talk about a jaw-drop moment.)

Carlo soon wanted spiritual direction, too. He wanted to know how he could get really close to Jesus, and he had one big wish: to receive the Eucharist. Fr. Carrai understood, and with the help of Archbishop Pasquale Macchi (secretary to St. Paul VI), he gave Carlo special permission to make his First Communion early.

And so, June 16, 1998, the big day, eventually came. Carlo was 7. The family drove to a convent of Romite cloistered nuns east of Milan. On the way up the hill to the monastery, a shepherd crossed the road with a white lamb. Carlo's dad hit the brakes, and Carlo's eyes lit up. The lamb! To him it was a sign from heaven. Beaming, he said, "My plan for my life is to always be united with Jesus."

When Carlo was 8, something truly amazing happened. During a church procession, Our Lady of Fátima appeared to him. Yes, you heard right. Carlo saw Mother Mary, wearing a large crown, walk up to him with his own eyes. She stopped in front of him, placed her heart in his chest, and told him to consecrate himself to her Immaculate Heart and to the Sacred Heart of Jesus. And do you know what? You can do the exact same thing! You probably won't see Our Lady with your eyes, but go ahead, right now, and ask her to come to you. Say: *"Mother Mary, please give me your heart. Today, I consecrate myself to your Immaculate Heart and to the Sacred Heart of Jesus."*

[Repeat the words now.]

If you mean what you just said, then the same thing that happened to Carlo also happened to you! You just received Mary's own heart inside of you. Isn't prayer so wonderful and powerful?

That same year when Carlo was 8 years old, the family went on vacation to Assisi, Italy—Carlo's favorite place in the whole wide world and the home of St. Francis of Assisi. When they were walking outside, a nun they'd never seen before came up to them and in summary, said, *"Your boy has a special mission in the Church."*

She was right—his mission was already unfolding. The Acutis family had no idea, but Carlo's life was meant to be a big, flashing road sign for kids and teenagers: "This is how you live a holy life in this modern world! This is how God created you to be!" Because, and let's be honest, we grown-ups don't always do a bang-up job teaching you how. So, God has given you Carlo as an example.

To be continued...

Now, go to sleep.

After Carlo's First Communion, he made it a habit to go to Mass every single day. When he received Jesus, he would whisper, "Jesus, make yourself at home!" (Kids, you should try that—Jesus loves house calls.) At age 6, he made a promise to Mary that he would pray a Rosary every day, and each morning he asked his guardian angel for his protection and guidance.

But Carlo didn't stop there. After his first Reconciliation, he went to the Sacrament of Confession, *once a week*. "We need to go often," he said, "It's like cleaning our soul. Even the smallest sin is like a string holding down a balloon." He wrote:

> In order to rise, a hot-air balloon needs to remove weights, just like how the soul needs to remove the little weights of venial sins in order to rise up to heaven. In the case of a mortal sin, the soul falls back to earth, and Confession is like the fire that makes the hot air balloon rise up again.

Carlo also spent time every day in Eucharistic Adoration—either before or after Mass. He used to say, "Before the sun, we become tan, but before the Eucharistic Jesus, we become holy." He invited people to Adoration with a challenge: "Do as I do, and you'll see what kind of revolution happens in you." He described it like sitting before a radiant sun—except this sun changes your soul, not your skin.

Carlo wrote a ton of beautiful things about Jesus in the Eucharist.[i] He was amazed that we live in a time when you can walk into a church and be right there with the Lord—and even receive Him in Communion. He said that people 2,000 years ago couldn't do that. They had to chase Jesus around Palestine, squeeze through crowds, and even climb trees like Zacchaeus! But we just step into the nearest church, and boom, "we have 'Jerusalem' right outside our front door."[ii] He wrote:

> Inside the Tabernacle, there is Life. There is Being. There is Eternity. There is the Infinite. It is a world apart. It is a new planet. It is a new start...[iii]

When Carlo was very young, St. Jacinta Marto visited him from heaven. St. Jacinta was one of the three shepherd children to whom Our Lady appeared in 1917, in Fátima, Portugal. Jacinta was only 7, at the time, her brother Francisco, 9, and their cousin Lucia dos Santos, 10. Jacinta and Francisco were canonized as saints in the Church, and the eldest became a nun and died in 2005, at the ripe age of 97! Carlo had a mystical connection with all of them, and, if you remember, with Our Lady of Fátima.

Jacinta came to tell him about one of the places where people can go after they die. Jacinta knew about it well because, you see, one of the 6 times that Our Lady appeared to the 3 Fátima children, she showed them hell. Apparently, Mother Mary wants her kids (and you're one of them) to know the truth about hell so you do everything you can to avoid it—and so you pray and make sacrifices so that others avoid it, too. After Jacinta saw what hell was like, she said to Lucia, "We must make many, many sacrifices and pray a lot for sinners so that no one will ever again have to go to that prison of fire where people suffer so much."

When St. Jacinta appeared to Carlo, she told him that no words on earth can describe the horror of hell. After that, Carlo thought a lot about life after death. "Mom," he said, "do you realize what it means to go to hell for all of eternity? Try to imagine being in a place forever and ever and ever and ever..."

Carlo was also struck by something he read in the memoirs of Sister Lucia, the eldest visionary. He learned that after the kids first saw Mary, they started asking her questions, just like you probably would. One was whether they would be brought to heaven. Our Lady answered that Lucia and Jacinta surely would be, but Francisco would need to pray many rosaries. Not long after Carlo read that, he told his parents, worried, "If Francisco, who was so good, so kind and simple, had to recite so many rosaries to go to heaven, how could I ever earn it, since in comparison I am much less saintly?" That's debatable.

In 2003, Carlo also had a dream involving Our Lady of Fátima. Angels with trumpets were spread across a blue sky that slowly began to fill with scary clouds. Then the scene changed, and Our Lady of Fátima appeared above Piazza San Pietro, which was full of a multitude of people enveloped in gray light. Our Lady said, "Difficult times await Christianity because of disobedience."

You can imagine that, at this point, Carlo really wanted to make it to heaven, bring people with him, and push away those scary clouds. The visionary Lucia came to Carlo in a dream, just a few days after she died, and she told him what he could do. She said that the practice of the First Five Saturdays could change the destiny of the world. (Now those are important words. Perk up.) On the first Saturday of the month, for five months in a row, Our Lady is asking us to:

1. Go to Confession (within 8 days before or after).
2. Receive Holy Communion.

3. Pray five decades of the Rosary.
4. Meditate for 15 minutes on the mysteries of the Rosary.

Carlo immediately began to share this devotion with friends and family, and through a website he created. He stressed how Our Lady said that the world will not have peace, unless we do these things—and do them with the intention of making reparation to her Immaculate Heart; this means with the desire that Mary's heart would be repaired and that no one would hurt her anymore.

Carlo also had a dream of Francisco, who asked him to make reparation and sacrifices so that people would love and honor the Eucharist more. To "make reparation" means to repair. Francisco was asking Carlo to help repair the harm done when people do not believe in or honor the True Presence of Jesus Christ in the Eucharist. You'll find out later how Carlo would answer Francisco's request in an extraordinary way.

All this contact with the Fátima apparitions made Carlo want to pray more and sacrifice more, just like the children of Fátima. He was convinced that everyone could not only be saved, but also have a constant, intimate relationship with Jesus, like he did. He told everyone to go to God with all of their needs. "He listens and answers," he'd say, "but you have to believe and have faith that this dialogue is possible and real."

To be continued...

Now go to sleep.

Now I'm going to invite you to take a journey upstream with Carlo. Why upstream? Because in order to be happy and holy in our modern world, you have to swim against a strong current. If you don't, you'll easily be swept downstream in the wrong direction. A lot of people end up like dead fish piled up on a sandbar downstream, dry and stinky with no water at the end of their lives. If you want to be like Carlo, that's not going to be you. Carlo was like a fish swimming the opposite direction, not just copying and doing what everybody else does, but swimming with the power of the Lord and ending up in the source: a big, beautiful, warm ocean of living water.

Let's look at some of Carlo's many swim strokes. (See the Endnotes for even more!)[iv]:

Carlo wanted an old bicycle rather than a new one and no more than one pair of shoes. He avoided fashions, trying to maintain a low profile. His peers sometimes teased him about his plain look, but that didn't faze him. He used to say, "Everything fades away, anyway. What will make us truly beautiful in the eyes of God is only the way in which we loved Him and how we loved our neighbors."

While riding his old bike to Mass and school from his family's upper-class apartment buildings in Mian, he would wave cheerfully to the doormen nearby, who were usually foreigners. "Ciao! Buona giornata!" *("Hi! Have a good day!")* he'd call out, and sometimes stop to chat with them and any janitors or maids he might run into. Others wondered why a young man from a well-off family would stop to chat with "those people."

Carlo had a contagious joy and playfulness about him, and he cared very deeply for his friends. One classmate from his Jesuit high school said: "If you were in a bad mood and spent time with him, it would fade away." After school he'd invite kids whose parents had just divorced or kids who were left out of the "cool" circles, over to his place. He hosted movie nights featuring his own home videos—starring the pets, of course, which cracked everyone up. When friends drifted off the road of truth, Carlo tapped the brakes—sometimes hard. Once, when his friends, along with his entire class, argued in class in favor of sins against marriage, sins against the body, and sins against life, he got upset and expressed his opposition to all of their positions. His friends defended themselves and looked confused.

On a family trip to Assisi, he gently told a group of kids he didn't even know to stop using God's name to curse. "You don't realize how much damage you're doing," he said. A little later at the town pool, he heard more blasphemy. One boy—whom Carlo had corrected earlier—got in his face and threatened him. Carlo didn't flinch. He quoted Padre Pio: "It is the most secure way to hell. It is the devil in your mouth." The kids went quiet, a little stunned. Words like that tend to stay with you.

At that same pool he saw two teenagers kissing in front of little children who looked embarrassed, amused, and very curious. No one did anything. Carlo got really angry and asked the lifeguard to tell them to stop—and he did. Guarding the innocence of children, he believed, was everybody's job. It disturbed him that so many people, grown-ups included, were doing the opposite.

Another time, Carlo's class silently watched as a young substitute teacher made fun of their classmate who had a hidden disability, which made it difficult for him to express himself. Carlo approached the teacher privately to explain the young man's issue, and the teacher apologized to Carlo many times.

Only a few things got Carlo to raise his voice. One was when friends bragged about visiting bad websites, reading things that damage the soul, or talking casually about doing things before marriage. He told them they were like marionettes in the movie Pinocchio—pulled by strings they couldn't see. "Someone wants to throw you straight into the fire," he warned. (And you know exactly which fire he meant.) Carlo wasn't judging; he was trying to cut the strings.

While kids herded themselves along, like sheep pretending to be their own shepherd, in order to see the latest movie, or watch the hottest show, Carlo's favorite forms of entertainment were cartoons and documentaries about animals. He never wanted to watch violent or vulgar films. If he saw impure advertisements on TV, he covered his eyes and immediately left the room, or asked his family to change the channel. Carlo's grandmother believed that Carlo practiced the virtue of purity to a heroic degree.

Just like many kids, Carlo was naturally drawn to technology and to video games. He liked some of the new consoles that came out in his time—Gameboy, PlayStation, GameCube, and Xbox. His mom set a limit as to how much he was allowed to play, but when he got a little older and read an article in an American newspaper—yes, he knew some English—he learned about physical dangers to the brain. Unlike most kids who don't care about or understand that technology is rewiring their brains, Carlo was concerned. He learned how videogame companies do research to make their games addicting so that they can make a boat load of money. Carlo wanted to protect himself, so he decided to a limit of one hour of gaming per week. Parents, kids, take this lesson to heart.

Carlo used to say that what is most lacking in today's world is a "critical spirit." We are easily misled by whatever the media or our peers tell us, and we forget to think for ourselves. "Everyone is born an original," he said, "but many die as photocopies."

When people asked Carlo if he had a girlfriend, he was none too happy. He thought middle school was too young to think about those things. "The Virgin Mary is the only woman in my life," he would say. When it came to Carlo's relationships with his friends, male or female, they were spontaneous and free-spirited. With girls, he was friendly, full of respect and affectionate. His family used to joke that he had a lot of sweethearts; but for him they were simply good friends. Carlo formed a particularly close friendship with one girl because of her interest in computer programming, and she asked him to give her some lessons. One day, when her boyfriend had just broken up with her,

Antonia Salzano Acutis (mother), Rajesh Mojur (housekeeper and friend), Carlo and Andrea Acutis (father)

this girl asked him to give her a "little kiss" because she was sad. Carlo gave her a little kiss on the cheek to cheer her up a bit. That was the only "little kiss" in his lifetime.

Carlo's mother once said, "In a certain sense, he was a boy from another time." Carlo could easily see how so much of what the world calls normal is really sin—and sin leaves the soul sad, ashamed, and bitter. He said happiness isn't looking like a famous star, collecting a bunch of cool stuff, and dumping our selfishness onto others. It is loving them like God does. God communicated to Carlo once that He was not happy with the vain, with those who were too attached to their image. In his photos, you see Carlo often wearing a backpack and holding a camera; he's ready to look outward and capture *God's* beauty in the Church and in nature—and share it with others. Carlo took no selfies. "Sadness is looking toward oneself," he would say. "Happiness is looking toward God."

Antonia wrote:

> Carlo was the opposite of unhappiness. I never heard him complain or grumble. On the contrary, he was always positive and optimistic, even in the most difficult of situations. He was full of energy and considered life to be an immense gift. He wanted to taste it with gusto in each moment because, as he said, "each moment that passes is one less moment we have to sanctify ourselves."

To be continued . . .
Now go to sleep.

Carlo's heart was like a mirror of Jesus' Heart: when Jesus felt joy or pain, Carlo often felt it, too. One day during a Sunday Mass at Santa Maria Segreta, when Carlo was only 9, the parish priest had the congregation renew their baptismal vows. After the Mass, Antonia saw that Carlo was very emotional. Antonia couldn't imagine what had upset him. The music had been beautiful; the incense behaved itself—so why the long face? "Why are you troubled?" she asked. He said our time on earth was not enough to thank Jesus for having given us baptism, and so many people do not realize what an infinite gift it is. He pointed out, almost in tears, that people seemed to be more interested in the presents, food, and the photographs than in the sacrament itself, which gives us back the divine life lost because of original sin.

A sadness came over Carlo's heart during a family visit to the picturesque town of Portofino on the Italian Riviera. The town is clustered around its small harbor and known for the colorfully painted buildings that line its shore. Since the late 19th century, Portofino has attracted tourism of the European aristocracy, and it is now a resort for the world's jet set.

As he looked around at the people in Portofino, he heard Jesus say two simple words to him, "I thirst": the same words that Jesus said on the Cross, just before He died. Jesus was thirsting for the souls of these rich people who were choosing material things over Him. Carlo said many times that "a step of faith is a step toward being, and a step away from having." Carlo explained that people who focus only on the material world and their possessions keep driving on the wrong side of the road. They're going in the opposite direction from their destination, and always at risk for crashing into someone, never getting to their true destination at all.

This pain in Carlo's heart over people not understanding what they were missing, along with the joy that he had in possessing it, naturally moved him to pray for others, learn his Faith, and bring people closer to Jesus Christ and His Church. As a little guy, Carlo made sure his female tutor didn't just do lessons with him but accompanied him at Mass. After meeting an extremely depressed woman who had been away from the Church for 40 years, he prayed for her and she not only healed from depression, but also went back to church, every day. At age 11, Carlo volunteered to be a teacher's assistant for catechism classes and ended up teaching classes by himself! Some of his friends converted or returned to Catholicism because of his example, and so did Rajesh and his friend; not to forget Carlo's own parents, who were his first converts.

Carlo came to call Rajesh "my trusted friend," and Rajesh came to call Carlo his "little catechist." Rajesh, who was from the island Mauritius off of southern Africa, said of his young teacher:

> Given how deeply religious Carlo was and the great faith that he had, it was normal that he often tended to give me lessons on Catholicism, since I was Hindu, from the priestly Brahmin caste. Carlo said that I would be happier one day if I became closer to Jesus, and he often taught me using the Bible, the Catechism of the Catholic Church, and stories of the saints. Carlo knew the catechism almost by memory, and he explained it so brilliantly that he was able to excite me about the importance of the sacraments...
>
> Carlo taught me what an authentic Christian life looked like and was an exceptional example of morality. I got baptized because Carlo infected me and struck me by his deep faith, his great charity, and his purity, which I always considered to be outside of the realm of normal, since such a young, beautiful, and rich boy would normally prefer to live a very different life.

One of the gifts that God gave Carlo was being a computer geek, and one of Carlo's favorite hobbies was researching Eucharistic miracles—real, supernatural events where Jesus shows Himself in the Eucharist. Carlo even made a website about them. His favorite? The one that happened in Lanciano, Italy, way back in 750 A.D. A monk was doubting whether the Host was really Jesus, and suddenly—bam—the bread turned into human heart tissue and the wine turned into blood, type AB. Scientists tested it centuries later in the 1970s and confirmed the miracle. And get this—the heart tissue is still alive today!

Carlo knew what to do with a keyboard and a calling. Between homework assignments and in the summers—sometimes staying up until 3 a.m.—he built online exhibits (you can explore them at www.carloacutis.com). At age 11, he began his crown jewel, "The Eucharistic Miracles of the World," which took two and a half years to complete. Then came "Angels and Demons," which told stories of saints and their encounters with the spirit world. After St. Jacinta's warning about hell shook him, he gathered testimonies for "Hell, Purgatory, and Heaven," to help people understand the afterlife. He also started "The Appeals of Our Lady," a project on Marian apparitions from around the world—but he never got to finish it. . .[v]

Carlo once said, "Every baptized person is a prophet,"—and he seemed to have an extra share. Antonia noticed that things Carlo would say that she didn't understand at the time, would eventually come true and be made clear. When Rajesh joked about going gray, Carlo would grin: "I will always be young." Since childhood he was strangely certain he would die from a burst vessel in his brain. It didn't frighten him. He wrote about death like a friend he expected to meet:

> ...We need to consider death not as the end of everything. It is not the end. It is not ruin. It is not the fatal conclusion. It is the transition to co-eternity. If we consider ourselves to be passing through this world, if we act as though we are temporary, if we aspire to what is Up Above, if we set our lives up based on the Beyond, if we base our existence on the Afterlife, then everything comes into order, everything becomes balanced, everything is oriented, everything is fed by hope...

He also wrote:

> ...If we consider life to be a trampoline towards Eternity, then death becomes a transition. It becomes a door. It becomes an in-between. It loses its drama. It loses its fatality. It loses its definitiveness. Exorcise death. Spiritualize death. Sanctify death. That is the secret. Then we will not think about, and we will not speak about, and we will not measure it in absolute terms, in terms of no return, of total destruction, but we will see death in the light, in the warmth and in the victory of the Risen Christ.[vi]

On the first Sunday of October 2006, when Carlo was 15, he started to feel unwell. On Thursday, October 5, he woke up with swollen glands, a sore throat and a fever, which usually took him more than a week to bounce back from, so his family didn't worry. They kept him company while he had dinner in his bedroom. Out of nowhere, he said, "I offer my suffering for the pope and for the Church, to skip purgatory and to go straight to heaven." They thought he was joking, like his normal self.

That same evening, Carlo wanted to recite the Prayer to Our Lady of the Rosary of Pompeii with his family, choosing the intentions himself: that they might be holy, skip purgatory, and after death, go straight to heaven.

A couple days later, Carlo's condition got worse. His body was swelling, due to internal hemorrhaging, and he had to go to the hospital. After taking some tests, the doctor said to him and his family: "There is no doubt that Carlo has been struck by type M3, or promyelocytic, leukemia." The doctor explained that it was a silent, serious, and very rare blood cancer, which destroys red blood cells faster than the body produces them. When he left the room, Carlo was able to stay calm in the face of the news. It was clear that the situation was critical, but he put himself in the arms of the Lord, Who conquered death. Smiling at his parents, he said, "God has given me a wake-up call!" With that, he lit up his parents' darkest hour.

Carlo was ready. He had written the following words a long time before:

> ... Existence should be a continuous preparation for death. . . When existence is attacked by disease or when the definitive sentence of death is pronounced, we must gladly adapt ourselves to Divine Will. Moreover, it is a very good exercise to unify ourselves intimately to the Passion and to the Death of the Lord. . . From a spiritual point of view, we need to feel and know that we are not permanent parts of the world. . . Our aim has to be the infinite and not the finite. The infinite is our homeland. Heaven has been waiting for us forever.

When Carlo was little, he had been very attached to his stuffed animals. The one he always treated with extra special care was his lamb, the lamb that somehow foreshadowed his destiny. A few months earlier, Carlo's mom had had a dream. In it, she saw a little lamb which was bleeding out and left to die, while a voice in Arabic said words that meant "sacrifice" or "victim." She did not know Arabic, so she looked up the exact words online and discovered their meaning.

In the hour of his sudden illness, he accepted his end like a meek lamb, offering himself to the Lord—a pleasing, unblemished sacrifice. Only hours after receiving the news of diagnosis, he was rushed by ambulance to a hospital in Monza, specializing in leukemia and lymphomas. As he was carried out of the vehicle, he said to his mother, "I'm not getting out of here alive. Prepare yourself." He would be there only four days.

"It had been years since I last saw a patient in that condition," one nurse said, "and I kept asking myself how he could keep himself from complaining about the pain, since he had swollen arms and legs that were full of fluid." And when he was asked, "How do you feel?" Carlo answered with his usual calmness. "Good, as always!" Half an hour later, he told his mom that he had a bit of a headache, and then he closed his eyes with a smile. He never opened them again. Carlo looked like he was only dozing, but he had fallen into a coma due to a cerebral hemorrhage that, over the course of a few hours, led to his death.

On October 12, 2006, Antonia told her mother, Luana, that Carlo had passed away. But she already knew because she had heard Carlo's voice tell her: "Grandma, I am in heaven with the angels. I am very happy. Don't cry, because I will always be there beside you."

Two months before his passing, Carlo had pulled out an old camera in his room and filmed himself, saying, "I've put on seventy kilograms [about 154 pounds] and am destined to die." He smiled and made a gesture of clapping his hands together in front of him, as if to say, "So be it." He wasn't sick at the time, he didn't have any diagnosis, he hadn't yet gained weight, but somehow, he knew.

Carlo was beatified on October 10, 2020, in Assisi, Italy, and was surely present from heaven for the occasion. Perhaps he was even wearing a heavenly backpack, since he had just taken off on a new adventure, this time, exploring paradise. A few months later, Carlo's mother had a dream. In the dream, he appeared to her and said, "Mamma, I will be beatified and then I will be canonized." And that's exactly what happened. On September 7, 2025, the Catholic Church declared Carlo Acutis a saint.

God made you to be a saint, too.

St. Carlo—and all the saints—will help you get there.

Now ask them to pray for you, and go to sleep!

APPENDIX

CARLO'S SAINT-MAKING "SECRETS"

When Carlo was 11, he began teaching catechism classes, as an assistant and then solo, and he created a plan for the kids to become saints. Actually, he created it for you, too. Here is what he wrote and wants you to follow:

> I want to tell you a few of my very special secrets that will help you quickly help you reach sainthood. Always remember that you, too, can become a saint! First, you have to want it with your whole heart, and if you do not have the desire yet, you must ask the Lord for it with insistence.
>
> Try to go to Mass every day and take Holy Communion.
>
> If you can, try to spend a few minutes in Eucharistic Adoration before the Tabernacle where Jesus is truly present. In this way, you'll see how your level of holiness increases!
>
> Remember to recite the Holy Rosary every day.
>
> Read a passage from Sacred Scripture every day.
>
> If you can, go to Confession every week, even for venial sins.
>
> Make promises often to God and the Virgin Mary to help others.
>
> Ask your guardian angel, who must become your best friend, for help.

NOTES

[i] "When a thin ray of light shines in a semi-dark room, you can see the dust in the air with your naked eye. In fact, it is the specks of dust found along the beam of light, themselves, which spread the light in every direction, just like how you can see the moon in the night sky. The same thing happens to our soul. During Eucharistic Adoration, we are struck by the light that radiates from the Eucharist. In this way, we are able to see all the "dust" that pollutes our soul and keeps us from progressing along the path to holiness, that we cannot normally see with our naked eye."

"Translation" for kids: Imagine this—when a thin ray of light sneaks into a dark room, suddenly you can see all the dust floating around. (And don't pretend your room doesn't have dust, kiddos—it does!) Those tiny specks only show up when the light hits them, spreading out in every direction, kind of like how you can spot the moon only at night. Carlo said the same thing happens to our souls in Adoration. When we sit before the Eucharist, the light of Jesus shines right into us and makes all the "dust" of our sins visible—stuff we normally wouldn't notice.

Carlo shared this with his pastor, Monsignor Gianfranco Poma:

> "The Lord is the only Person Whom we don't have to ask if He's available. I can always confide something in Him. I can also complain or question Him in silent moments and tell Him the things that I don't understand. Then I find within me some word He sends me some passage from the Gospel that cloaks me in security and confidence."

[ii] Carlo wrote, "People who lived alongside Jesus could not eat His Body and drink His Blood, like we can. They could not do Eucharistic Adoration, through which Jesus transfigures us and makes us more like Him...

If we truly reflect, we are much, much luckier than those who lived more than 2,000 years ago with Jesus in Palestine. The apostles, the disciples, and the people of those times could meet Him, touch Him, talk to Him, but they were limited by space and time. Many had to travel for miles on foot to meet Him, but it was not always possible to approach Him because He was always surrounded by crowds. Just think of Zacchaeus who climbed a tree to see him. All we need to do, however, is go into the nearest church, and we have 'Jerusalem' right outside our front door!"

[iii] Carlo wrote: "The Tabernacle must become everyone's home, everyone's residence, a place where people can meet...

This visit must be qualified by worship. Worshiping. We recognize that we are before the One God. The distance is infinite, even though the Tabernacles is a few meters away...

Using words of dialogue with an Absolute Interlocutor. Reflecting... that you are before the Eucharist. The visit passes through the respectful feelings of worship interwoven with faith in the One God, hope in One God, and love for the One God. We also confess, climbing up to the top to the Commandments of Sinai and continuing along the commandments of the Church and walking down the paths of the duties of one's state of life. And then it becomes opportune to recite the Lord's prayer, Hail Mary, Glory Be, the Guardian Angel Prayer... The visit comes to a close. We submit the day's plans to the Lord, professing that everything will be done for the glory of God. The farewell can be externalized with the use of a few short prayers, such as, 'Oh Jesus, make me love you even more.' 'Lord, take me as I am and make me as you wish.' 'I will try to offend you less.' 'Lord, I abandon myself to you.' And similar prayers."

[iv] A food-lover with a sweet tooth, Carlo was known to stock up on his favorite focaccia and enjoy his mother's homemade desserts, but even so, according to his mom, he controlled his portions and didn't even snack. The non-snacking part is probably one of the biggest miracles I've ever heard of. That virtue, right there, is enough for official sainthood.

Carlo's virtue of self-restraint was evident at a young age. When Carlo was around 8, he put on a few pounds; while vacationing seaside, the family went overboard with Italian pizza and gelato.

When they returned home, Carlo moderated his eating on his own and immediately lost weight, making small sacrifices to help the souls in purgatory and for the Virgin Mary. He also made sacrifices by not watching his favorite movies.

Worrying about his mom's health, Carlo hid his desserts from her because he knew if she saw them lying around, they would be gobbled up. Wanting to see her healthy, he also took her on walks to help her lose weight. He did the same with Rajesh because he was diabetic.

One year, during summer vacation in Assisi, Carlo received the grace of feeling the Passion of Christ inside of him. It took him a long time to collect himself. After that, he began to do the Stations of the Cross, and he started to make wooden crosses with the branches that he and his mom found on their walks in the woods of La Verna, where St. Francis of Assisi first experienced the stigmata—the wounds of Christ in his body. On some of the crosses of wood, Carlo would write a few words, such as something Pope John Paul II said in his inaugural Mass on October 22, 1978: "Do not be afraid. Open wide the doors for Christ." He hoped that people would find these symbols out in nature and think of how Jesus had died for them.

Carlo knew that anything in excess could easily turn into sin. When Antonia eyed a name-brand bottle of sunscreen that cost around 50 Euros (about 70 dollars at the time), he was scandalized by the price. He didn't like how his mom could be spendthrift and gave her a lecture on how extra money spent like that was money that could have helped the poor.

Carlo loved his family's housekeeper, Rajesh, but he wanted him to be less materialistic. Starting very young, Carlo would write letters to Jesus, asking him to change Rajesh's heart. One day, Carlo was invited to lunch at his friend's house, whose family was rich and famous. Afterward, Rajesh bombarded him with questions, trying to get the scoop on the family and their riches. Carlo pretended not to hear, but Rajesh kept going. Fascinated and excited, he wouldn't let up. After too many questions, Carlo kindly replied in a funny, gruff, Roman accent, that the house of the celebrities had a room, a kitchen, and a bathroom.

v Carlo's parents finished the website. You can see Carlo's websites here: www.carloacutis.com.

vi In an interview shared on EWTN, in a Documentary called, "I Am with You," Rajesh shared even more:

> I'm Rajesh, and I come from Mauritius [an island off of southern Africa]. I started working with the Acutis family, with Carlo. At that time, he was very young. He was full of affection. After nursery school, he started school with the Marceline Sisters. I'd sometimes bring him there, and then he asked if I could take him into the church to have a little sort of meditation by the Tabernacle. I didn't know anything. I'd wonder what was going on. I could understand if he were an adult… Then he told me, "What's inside is the Body of Jesus, present in Body, Blood, Soul and Divinity."
>
> I said, "But Carlo, how is it possible?" And he would then slowly explain it to me during the time I took him to school. Every day he told me the same thing. I wasn't a Christian. I come from a Hindu—a Brahmin family. And my father was a so-called Pandit and a kind of priest. He had knowledge of of the language of Sanskrit. It's very rare, almost impossible, for a Brahmin to convert. The teaching I had from Carlo was more than from my father. I can say he was my spiritual master. All of his actions struck me right in the heart. Then he said to me, "The Lord lives in the heart, too."
>
> Then, as he started to grow up, I felt that when he went to Mass and took Communion, he didn't force me. Carlo explained the importance of the Eucharist to me, how it causes people to live, because this world is full of temptations. He explained

how they can come in the form of clothes, s- -, alcohol, TV. He said that this is how the devil enters your life, and you can't face the situation alone.

And so, when he started to explain to me the Word of God, the Bible, he did so with sweetness. It was as if we'd already gone up to heaven. And he told me what heaven is like, how to live, even how to live with the Lord. It was as if I'd already arrived. I was happy. Then I also had dreams about Jesus, the Lord, and the Virgin Mary. Then I started to tell Carlo about it. I asked him, "How can I have these dreams?" He told me, "Jesus loves you, Rajesh." Then I had myself baptized. It was 1999.

(YouTube: "I Am With You - A Documentary on Carlo Acutis," posted by EWTN, August 23, 2025, https://www.youtube.com/watch?v=dUpqQneSOFM, accessed August 25, 2025)

WHO WROTE WHAT

Fr. Frank Lee wrote the stories of St. Joseph, St. Paul, St. Patrick, St. Francis de Sales, St. Edmund Campion, St. Joan of Arc, St. Gerard Majella, St. Anthony of Padua, St. Clement Maria Hofbauer, St. Benedict Labre, and St. John Bosco.

Christine Watkins wrote the stories of St. Kateri Tekakwitha, Servant of God Julia Greeley, Blesseds Maria & Luigi Beltrame Quattrocchi, St. Catherine Labouré, Venerable Francis Xavier Nguyễn Văn Thuận, and St. Carlo Acutis.

∽ NOTE TO THE READER ∽

AMAZON REVIEWS

If you were graced by this book, would you kindly post a short review of *Bedtime with the Saints: Featuring Saint Carlo Acutis* on www.Amazon.com? Your support will help create the next generation of saints in our world!

To leave a short review, go to Amazon.com and type in *Bedtime with the Saints: Featuring Saint Carlo Acutis*. Click on the book and scroll down the page. Underneath "Customer Reviews," click on "Write a customer review." Thank you, in advance, for your kindness.

OTHER BOOKS
BY QUEEN OF PEACE MEDIA

GO TO:

www.QueenofPeaceMedia.com/catholic-bookstore

FOR VIDEO TRAILERS:

https://www.queenofpeacemedia.com/great-catholic-books

ALL OTHER ITEMS:

sacramentals, brochures, and more
www.QueenofPeaceMedia.com/shop

Books are available through
QueenofPeaceMedia.com and Amazon.com in
Print, Ebook, and Audiobook formats

THE MIRACULOUS MEDAL

PENDANT OF POWER

"The graces will be abundant for those who wear it with confidence."
- **Our Lady of the Miraculous Medal to St. Catherine Labouré**

Learn why St. Maximilian Kolbe called It his Silver Bullet, why St. Mother Theresa called It her Medal of Charity, and why the world calls It Miraculous. Take a tour through the last two centuries of the most amazing collection of Miraculous Medal testimonies ever written. Discover how one small piece of metal has helped the sick recover, the blind see, the disbelieving come to faith, the desperate find hope, and even converted a High-Wizard satanist in a matter of minutes.

Free Miraculous Medals in bulk and Evangelization Packets, with cords sold at cost, are available now at **QueenofPeaceMedia.com**.

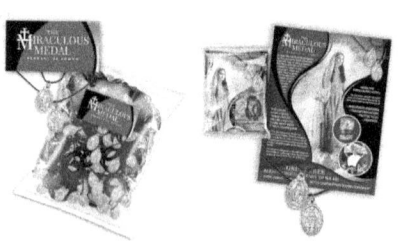

MARY'S MANTLE CONSECRATION
A SPIRITUAL RETREAT FOR HEAVEN'S HELP

Endorsed by **Archbishop Salvatore Cordileone** and **Bishop Myron J. Cotta**

(See www.MarysMantleConsecration.com)

"Now more than ever, we need a miracle. Christine Watkins leads us through a 46-day self-guided retreat that focuses on daily praying of the Rosary, a Little fasting, and meditating on various virtues and the seven gifts of the Holy Spirit, leading to a transformation in our lives and in the people on the journey with us!"

- **Fr. Sean O. Sheridan, TOR**
Former President,
Franciscan University,
Steubenville

"I am grateful to Christine Watkins for making this disarmingly simple practice, which first grew in the fertile soil of Mexican piety, available to the English-speaking world."

- **Archbishop Salvatore Cordileone**

THE WARNING

TESTIMONIES AND PROPHECIES OF THE ILLUMINATION OF CONSCIENCE
Revised and Expanded Second Edition

Endorsed by Msgr. Ralph J. Chieffo, Fr. John Struzzo, Fr. Berdardin Mugabo, and more...

The Warning has been an Amazon #1 best-seller, ever since its release. In the book are authentic accounts of saints and mystics of the Church who have spoken of a day when we will all see our souls in the light of truth, and fascinating stories of those who have already experienced it for themselves.

"*With His divine love, He will open the doors of hearts and illuminate all consciences.*

Every person will see himself in the burning fire of divine truth. It will be like a judgment in miniature."
- Our Lady to Fr. Stefano Gobbi of the Marian Movement of Priests

SHE WHO SHOWS THE WAY

HEAVEN'S MESSAGES FOR OUR TURBULENT TIMES

Endorsed by Ramón C. Argüelles, STL, Archbishop-Emeritus

"A great turning point in the fate of your nation...will soon be upon you..."
- Mary's message of August 4, 1993

#1 AMAZON BEST-SELLER

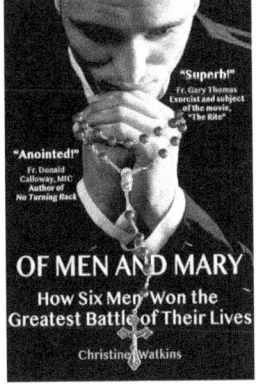

OF MEN AND MARY

HOW SIX MEN WON THE GREATEST BATTLE OF THEIR LIVES

"ANOINTED!"
-Fr. Donald Calloway, MIC

"Of Men and Mary is superb... miraculous, heroic, and truly inspiring."
-Fr. Gary Thomas
Exorcist and subject of the movie, "The Rite."

TRANSFIGURED

PATRICIA SANDOVAL'S ESCAPE FROM DRUGS, HOMELESSNESS, AND THE BACK DOORS OF PLANNED PARENTHOOD

Endorsed by Archbishop Salvatore Cordileone & Bishop Michael C. Barber, SJ

"Are you ready to read one of the most powerful conversion stories ever written? I couldn't put this book down!"
- Fr. Donald Calloway, MIC

WINNING THE BATTLE FOR YOUR SOUL

JESUS' TEACHINGS THROUGH MARINO RESTREPO, A ST. PAUL FOR OUR CENTURY

This book contains some of the most extraordinary teachings that Jesus has given to the world through Marino Restrepo, teachings that will profoundly alter and inform the way you see your ancestry, your past, your purpose, and your future.

"This book is an authentic jewel of God."
- **Internationally renowned author, María Vallejo-Nájera**

SERVANT OF GOD FRANK DUFF

FOUNDER OF THE LEGION OF MARY

"This layman from Dublin, Ireland, multiplied a group of thirteen women into three million people—into the largest Catholic lay apostolate the world has ever known: The Legion of Mary. Discover the spiritual jewel of the story of Servant of God, Frank Duff."

FREE E-book:
www.QueenofPeaceMedia.com/frank-duff

IN LOVE WITH TRUE LOVE

THE UNFORGETTABLE STORY OF SISTER NICOLINA

This book is a privileged view into not only a charming soul and an enthralling love story, but into the secrets of Love itself.

**To be notified of new and upcoming
Queen of Peace Media books,
sign up for our occasional newsletter:**

www.QueenofPeaceMedia.com/newsletters

www.ingramcontent.com/pod-product-compliance
Lightning Source LLC
Chambersburg PA
CBHW081444070526
44586CB00019B/2222